CANDY CONTAINERS
FOR COLLECTORS
Debra S. Braun

Schiffer Publishing Ltd®

4880 Lower Valley Road, Atglen, PA 19310 USA

Disclaimer

All of the pictures, graphics, and photos compiled herein are intended to heighten the awareness of candy containers and related products. This book is in no way intended to infringe on the intellectual property rights of any party. All products, brands, characters, and names represented are trademarks or registered trademarks of their respective companies.

The information in this book was derived from the author's independent research and was not authorized, furnished or approved by the companies represented.

Copyright © 2002 by Debra S. Braun
Library of Congress Control Number: 2001093197

Designed by "Sue"
Type set in ShelleyAllegro BT/Souvenir Lt BT

ISBN: 0-7643-1482-3
Printed in China
1 2 3 4

Published by Schiffer Publishing Ltd.
4880 Lower Valley Road
Atglen, PA 19310
Phone: (610) 593-1777; Fax: (610) 593-2002
E-mail: Schifferbk@aol.com
Please visit our web site catalog at **www.schifferbooks.com**
We are always looking for people to write books on new and related subjects. If you have an idea for a book please contact us at the above address.

This book may be purchased from the publisher.
Include $3.95 for shipping.
Please try your bookstore first.
You may write for a free catalog.

In Europe, Schiffer books are distributed by
Bushwood Books
6 Marksbury Ave.
Kew Gardens
Surrey TW9 4JF England
Phone: 44 (0) 20 8392-8585; Fax: 44 (0) 20 8392-9876
E-mail: Bushwd@aol.com
Free postage in the U.K., Europe; air mail at cost.

Dedication

This book is dedicated to all of the
"sweet talkers" out there.

Collector's Corner

Donna Ambeau's collection is featured in Chapter Five. She began purchasing candy containers for her three children. Whenever she stopped at the local grocery store, she purchased four (of the same) candy containers. In the early 1980s, they cost 25 cents each. The first candy container that she bought was a plastic coffin manufactured by Fleer Corp. She can remember her children putting together the bone-shaped candy skeleton, "Mr. Bones."

The storeowner recognized her cravings for candy and told her when new items arrived. Donna's original plan was to give each child a candy container and stash one away for a "special treat." She had intended on giving the extra ones away for recognition. But, her children were content with just "looking through them and putting them back" in the box. Eventually, the accumulation was deemed as being *her* collection.

It is interesting that candy containers reflect our lifestyles. We see advertisements (i.e., Where's the Beef?) and product evolution (i.e., a radio to a boom box to a CD player). Donna's favorite candy containers have food related themes (i.e., TV dinner "Windy's," and "Zilly-Zereal"). She also likes the early plastic containers that have relevant candy shapes (i.e., Garbage can complete with trash-shaped candy).

Donna's family continues to search for unusual containers (i.e., Barfo and Lobster Egg gum). Since the photography was completed for this book, 50 more candy containers have been added to her assortment. It is estimated that she now has over 300 pieces. In addition to candy containers, she also collects paperweights. Donna is a Registered Nurse who resides in Webster, New York with her husband (and two cats).

Contents

Acknowledgments

I would like to extend a special thanks to my parents, Donna and Richard Ambeau, Cathy and Matt Sinacola, Mark Coté, Tracey Curry, Peter and Nancy Schiffer, Doug Congdon-Martin (Editor), Bruce Waters (Cover Photographer), Sue Taylor (Book Layout), Tina Skinner (Public Relations), Terry Whitmeyer, and the staff at Wink One Hour Photo. All of these people were instrumental in the development of this book. I really appreciate all of their guidance and support.

I would also like to thank my co-workers and friends for believing in me and making me smile.

Photography by: TOBY

Introduction

You might think that I'm *Bonkers*, but our lives revolve around candy in this land of *Good & Plenty*. Have you ever … Dreamed of going to *Mars* or the *Milkyway?* Wished that you had more *PEZ-zazz?* Searched for a *Sugar Daddy* (or *Sweet Tarts*) on *5th Avenue?* I can hear your *Snickers.* But, wouldn't we all like to live *Carefree* and earn a *100 Grand Payday?* One thing is *Certain*, I should have been a dentist. Did you know that the candy industry generates yearly revenues of $23 Billion? Yes. It's the "sweet tooth" and nothing but the "tooth!" On average, each American consumes 12 pounds of candy per year. Advertisers entice people to buy their product through name recognition, catchy slogans, and innovative packaging. Today, candy enthusiasts are eager to add vintage and modern containers to their collections.

The word candy is derived from many languages (i.e., qandi (Arabic), zucchero candi (Italian), sucre candy (French), and sugre candi (English)). Most people think of a candy bar as being chocolate, however the term candy actually means "cane sugar." The origins of chocolate can be traced back to the Aztec Indians. They used to serve their emperor, Montezuma, a warm drink called, "xocoatl." It was made from beans that were harvested from the tropical cacao tree. When Spanish explorer Hernan Cortes and his crew traveled to Mexico, they were offered some xocoatl (1519). Since the Spaniards found it to be bitter tasting, they added cane sugar, cinnamon, and vanilla. **Note:** The word cocoa is a rough translation based on the cacao tree.

At first, only the affluent could afford liquid "drinking" chocolate. However, revolutionary inventions (i.e., steam engine (1730) and cacao press (1828)) reduced costs, making chocolate available to all. During the 19th century, chemists and confectioners united in the pursuit of making an incredible edible. In 1847, England's J.S. Fry and Sons (currently, Cadbury) introduced a solid "eating" chocolate that had a smooth velvety consistency. Ten years later, Switzerland's Daniel Peter (candymaker) and Henri Nestle (chemist) created solid "condensed milk" chocolate. By 1894, America's Milton Hershey perfected his recipe for solid "fresh whole milk" chocolate.

It's interesting that Milton Hershey didn't believe in advertising his product. He was confident that it would sell based on content, identity, and value. Hershey's candy bar wrappers were red and black before 1903. After that, he changed them to maroon and silver. Other companies relied on store displays and candy containers to lure in potential customers. One of the first glass candy containers was launched at the Centennial Exposition in Philadelphia, Pennsylvania (1876). It was in the shape of the Liberty Bell; manufactured by Croft, Wilbur and Co. **Note:** Glass containers were produced until the 1960s. However, they were discontinued when manufacturing became too costly.

In the beginning of the 19th century, "paper" boxes were traditionally used for storing hats, furs, collars, and pills. By 1865, the National Biscuit Company (Nabisco) began to use "cardboard" packaging for perishable products. Candy manufacturers utilized cardboard boxes for housing chocolate, gum, taffy, and peppermint sticks. Since we live in a "disposable" world, candy boxes are in limited supply. Collectors often look for vintage boxes that have colored illustrations of children, teddy bears, rabbits, and fairy tale scenes. In addition, boxes decorated with cloth, linen, and lace accents are also desirable. **Note:** The Swiss created the heart-shaped box for Valentine's Day in 1913.

In 1810, Frenchman Nicholas Appert preserved food in tin cans for his war bound troops. Napoleon Bonaparte was pleased with his efforts and awarded him a prize. Surprisingly, he didn't patent the idea. During the same year, a patent application for a similar "tin can" invention was filed and granted to British inventor, Peter Durand. During the Civil War, tin can manufacturers Libby and Van Camp utilized mechanized canning. It was common for early cans to be decorated with decals, stenciling, and paper labels. In the 1870s, color lithography was introduced. Designs were indicative of the Victorian lifestyle (i.e., graceful women, angelic children, and pastoral scenery). By the early 20th Century, general stores displayed tin candy pails on their countertops.

Wartime shortages in the 1940s, encouraged candy container manufacturers to utilize plastic/paper instead of glass/tin. The word plastic was derived from the Greek word *plastikos*. It means to mold or form. The evolution of plastic is as follows: cellulose (1867), casein (1897), and Bakelite resin (1907). When manufacturers discovered the flexible properties of plastic, items like candy containers and jewelry flooded the market. Consumers welcomed the wide variety of colors, textures, and shapes. Even today, plastic candy containers dominate the market. Some of the leading manufacturers are: Amurol Confections, Mars Candy, Inc., Cap Candy/OddzOn Inc., PEZ Candy, Inc., and The Topps Co., Inc.

Thousands of candy, gum, and snacks debut annually. Amurol Confections determine the marketing trends for their products "out of the mouths of babes." Their market research facility, the Candy Tasters Club, asks 3,000 children (per year) to rate new concepts, prototypes, and flavors. This type of research is invaluable. As we all know, most kids will not "sugarcoat" their answers. Simply put, a product will either be "flip" or "flop." According to Amurol's website (www.bubblegum.com), "if the children don't like it, it doesn't get made."

If you feel like a "kid in a candy store," you're not alone. The Candy Container Collectors of America publishes a newsletter called the "Candy Gram." It is an excellent resource for networking with other collectors. In addition, they sponsor an annual convention in Eastern Pennsylvania. The event features a candy swap, banquet, auction, and seminar. For more information logon to: www.candycontainer.org. Or, send a self addressed stamped envelope to: Betty MacDuff - Membership Chairman, 2711 DeLaRosa Street, The Villages, Florida 32159.

Helpful Hints

Searching for candy containers at toy shows, flea markets, and on-line auctions is challenging and fun. You never know what you are going to find. It is important to understand that the prices for candy memorabilia will fluctuate according to their condition, supply, and demand. You should purchase an object because you like it, not for an investment. This book is intended to heighten your awareness of candy collectibles and their approximate values in excellent to mint condition on a secondary market. Most of the items shown in this book were produced between 1970-2001.

There are several things to consider before purchasing an object. For example: Is it in good condition? Are all of the pieces complete? Is it rare and hard to find? It is my recommendation is to inspect each item thoroughly. Especially look for chips, hairline cracks, and paint peeling.

Tip 1. One way to identify a hairline crack in an object is to hold it up to a light. The hairline crack should stick out instantly even if it has been repaired.

Tip 2. To feel a chip easily, gently move your finger around the entire surface of an object.

Tip 3. Price tags sometimes get so sticky that they can ruin any object. If you are considering on making a purchase, you may want to ask the vendor to carefully remove his price tag so that the exact condition is disclosed.

Tip 4. Sunlight can cause permanent discoloration on plastic if an object is exposed over a significant period of time.

Tip 5. If an item is made up of multiple parts, take the time to make sure that all pieces are accounted for.

Tip 6. The following dates may be helpful to determine the age of a container: ingredients listed on label (1940), sterilization label (1957), nutrition facts label (1994). Also, remember that zip codes weren't introduced into the USA until 1963.

Tip 7. Educate yourself on bootleg and reproduction containers. Always look for licensing and copyright information. For example: PEZ Candy, Inc. has never produced a set of dispensers that depict the rock band, Kiss. If you ever see these, look at them carefully. Each Kiss dispenser is painted over a Wonder Woman © DC Comics base. Gene Simmons' hairline is actually painted on top of Wonder Woman's crown.

Keep in mind that if a slight imperfection is in an inconspicuous place, then the object may still look nice on a display.

Most of us are on a budget, so every penny counts. Once you have established what type of condition the object is in, you should also estimate a fair price. Lately, it appears as though glass items in particular are commanding extremely high prices. I usually rate the object first on rarity, then on condition. I would probably buy a rare object at any price even with slight imperfections. However, if an object is common, I may wait until I can find it somewhere in mint condition.

The matrix below can help to estimate the condition of an object on a scale from 1 to 10 and price it accordingly.

Grade	Condition	Definition	Price Example
1-4	Poor	Item shows major signs of wear. No tags and/or packaging present (i.e., Noticeably broken, reglued or discolored). No candy.	$1-4
5	Fair	Item shows minor signs of wear and has some missing components. No tags and/or packaging present (i.e., Missing container closure). No candy.	$5
6	Good	Item has been used and shows minor signs of wear. No tags and/or packaging present (i.e., Small chip in an inconspicuous area or very slight crazing). No candy.	$6
7	Very Good	Item has been used but is still pristine. No tags and/or packaging present. A trace of candy is left.	$7
8	Excellent	Item has been gently used but is still pristine. Original tags and/or packaging may be ripped or damaged. Still has less than half of candy.	$8
9	Near Mint	Item has been gently used but is still pristine. Original tags and/or packaging may be unsealed and slightly worn. Still has more than half of candy.	$9
10	Mint	Item has never been used and is pristine. Original tags are present and/or packaging is sealed from the factory. Complete with candy.	$10

One last thing, vendors at flea markets and toy shows expect you to barter on prices. Don't be shy! If an object is priced too expensive for the condition that it is in, let the vendor know in a diplomatic manner. If your criticism is warranted, the vendor will often reduce his asking price. Best of luck in your hunting endeavors!

Chapter One: Glass

Figure, glass. Manufacturer unknown, 1920s. Marked Germany. 2.75" tall. $100-150.

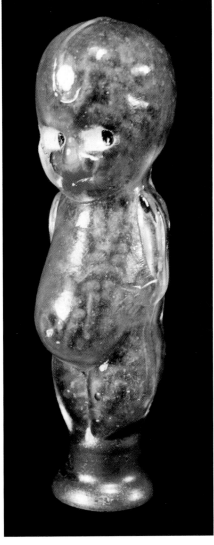

Figure, glass. Manufacturer unknown, 1920s. 2.25" tall. $100-150.

Santa, glass. Manufacturer unknown, N/A. 4" tall. $150-200.

Spark Plug © KFS, glass. Manufacturer unknown, 1920s. 3" tall. $100-150.

Dog, glass. J.C. Crosetti, Co., 1960s. 2.75" tall. $15-20.

Rabbit, glass. J.H. Millstein, Co., 1940s. 6.5" tall. $30-45.

Dog, glass. T.H. Stough Co., 1950s. 3.25" tall. $5-10.

Right:
Telephone, glass. Victory Glass Co., 1940s. 5" tall.
$50-75. **Note:** The wood mouthpiece that came with
the candlestick shaped telephone is not shown.

Telephone, glass. J.H. Millstein
Co., 1940s. Caption: "Tot
Telephone." 2.5" tall. $30-45.

Telephone, glass. J.C. Crosetti Co., 1950s. 1.75" tall. $30-45.

Die, glass. Brandle & Smith Co., N/A. Caption: "Bristol/Diced/Mints." 3.25" tall. $20-35.

Telephone & Lantern combo, glass. Allen Mitchell Products, 1970s. 5" tall. $10-15.

Baby bottle, glass. T.H. Stough Co., N/A. 2.5" tall.
$20-35.

Lantern, glass. J.C. Crosetti Co., 1960s. 2.25"
tall. $20-35.

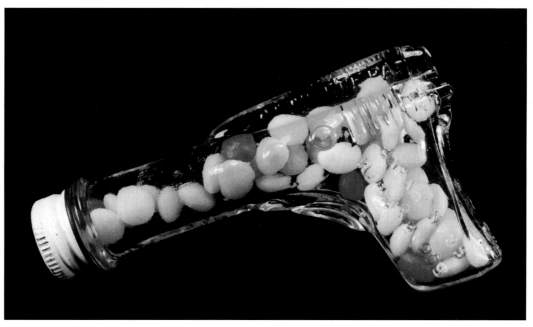

Gun, glass. Manufactured by
T.H. Stough Co., 1960s. 2"
tall. $20-35.

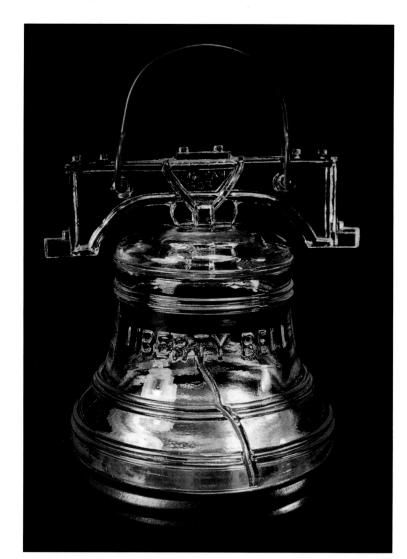

Liberty bell, glass. Westmore Glass Co., 1920s. 3.5" tall (w/o handle). $40-55.

U.S. Military hat, glass. Victory Glass Co., 1940s. 3" in diameter. $20-35.

Tank, glass. Victory Glass Co.,
N/A. 2" tall. $50-75.

Battleship, glass. Victory Glass
Co., 1940s. 2" tall. $30-45.

Train, glass. Victory Glass Co.,
1930s. Caption: "Curved line
888." 2.25" tall. $50-75.

Train, glass. Manufacturer unknown, 1920s. Complete with lithographed metal closure. 3" tall. $100-150.

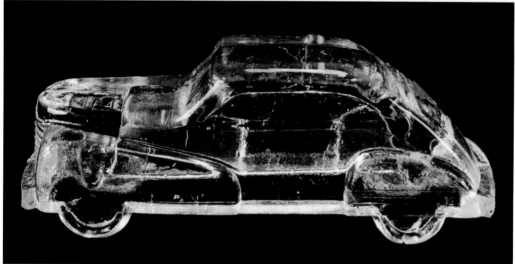

Car, glass. Victory Glass Co., 1940s. 1.75" tall. $20-35.

Car, glass. Fresh Pack Candy Co., N/A. 2" tall. $5-10.

Chapter Two: Cardboard

Telephone, cardboard. Manufacturer unknown, N/A. Caption: "Hello Central." 4.5" tall. $100-150.

Box, cardboard. Manufacturer unknown, N/A. Caption: "Collectionnez Confectionnez." Complete with punch out mouth and eyes. 3.75" tall. $5-10.

Luggage, cardboard. Manufacturer unknown, N/A. 1" tall. $50-75. **Note:** The leather strap that came with the luggage is not shown.

Box, cardboard. Manufacturer unknown, N/A. Caption: "Little Miss Muffet sat on a tuffet eating curds and whey." 4.25" tall. $10-15.

Box, cardboard. Manufacturer unknown, N/A. Caption: "Old King Cole was a merry old soul - a merry old soul was he." 4.25" tall. $10-15.

Box, cardboard. Manufacturer unknown, N/A. Caption: "Tom Tom the Piper's son stole a pig and away he run." 4.25" tall. $10-15.

Box, cardboard. Manufacturer unknown, 1930s. Marked France. Caption: "Fruits Confits." 4" tall. $40-55.

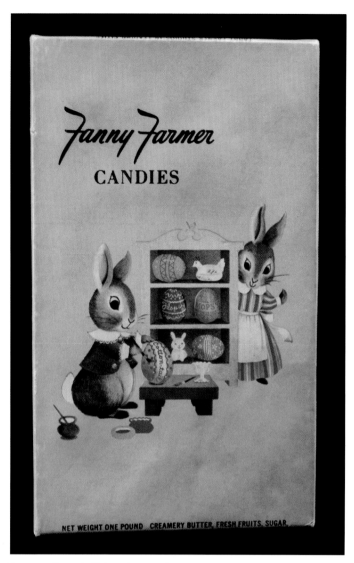

Box, cardboard. Fanny Farmer Candies, 1950s. Rabbit with a sprinkling can. 3.25" tall. $10-15.

Box, cardboard. Fanny Farmer Candies, 1950s. Rabbits in front of an egg-filled cupboard. 6" tall. $15-20.

Box, cardboard. Fanny Farmer Candies, 1950s. Rabbit sitting in a rocking chair. Under 4.75" tall. $10-15 each.

Box, cardboard. Fanny Farmer Candies, 1990s. Caption: "A Happy Easter." 5" tall. $5-10.

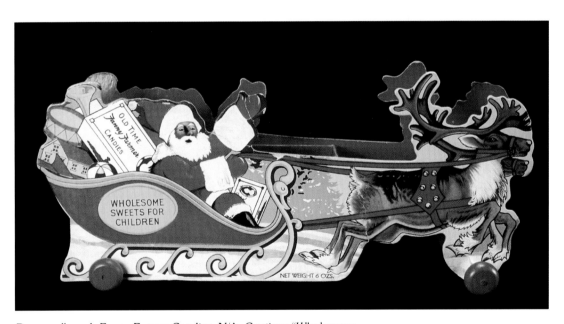

Box, cardboard. Fanny Farmer Candies, N/A. Caption: "Wholesome sweets for children" Santa in a sled. 10.5" tall. $150-200.

Box, cardboard. Game Makers, N/A. Santa on a motorcycle. 10" tall. $100-150.

Box, cardboard. Container Corporation of America, 1930s. Santa in a sled. 3" tall. $5-10.

Box, cardboard. Maillard's New York, 1900s. Caption: "Excellence assorted bon bons and chocolates." Complete with matching doilies. 4" tall. $20-35.

Box, cardboard. Liberty Orchards Co., N/A. Caption: "Aplets. The confection of the fairies." 6.5" long. $40-55.

Box, cardboard. F.N. Burt, N/A. Caption: "Fine Confections." 7.25" long. $5-10.

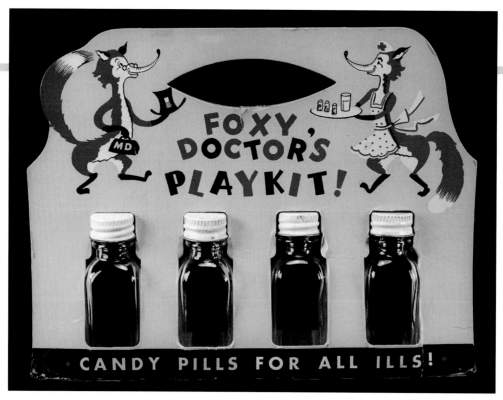

Play kit, cardboard. Empire Products, Inc., 1950s. Caption: "Foxy Doctor's Play Kit." 5.75" tall. $100-150.

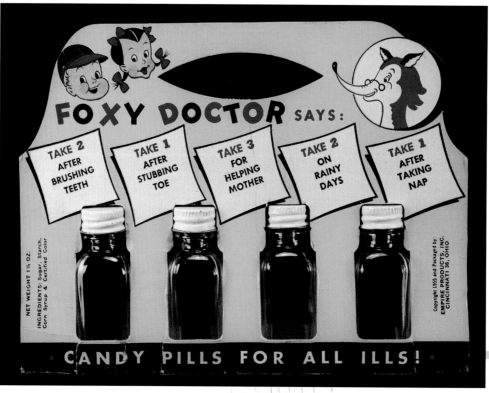

Flip side of the Foxy Doctor's Play Kit. Captions: "Take 2 after brushing teeth. Take 1 after stubbing toe. Take 3 for helping mother. Take 2 on rainy days. Take 1 after taking nap."

Chapter Three: Paper Mache (Plus)

Santa, paper mache. Alexander Wiede-Druck U.
Papierhaus, N/A. Santa holding a Christmas tree. 7" tall.
$300+.

Santa, paper mache. Manufacturer unknown, N/A.
Marked Germany. 14" tall. $600+. ***Note:*** The
dolls were not part of the original packaging.

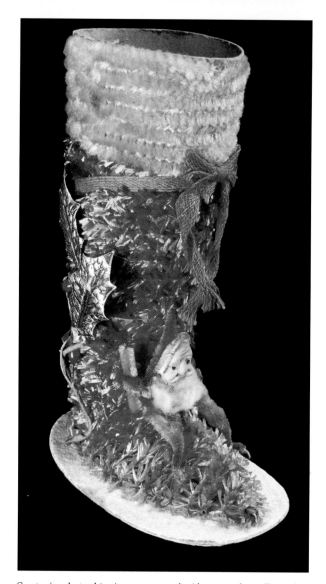

Santa (and stocking), paper mache/decorated cardboard.
Manufacturer unknown, N/A. 5.5" tall. $50-75.

Santa, celluloid with mesh body.
Manufacturer unknown, N/A. 7"
tall. $100-150. **Note:** The candy
shown is not original.

Santa (and house), paper mache/
decorated cardboard. Manufacturer
unknown, N/A. Marked Germany.
3" tall. $100-150.

Santa (and car), celluloid with mesh body/decorated cardboard. Manufacturer unknown, N/A. Marked Japan. 5" tall. $150-200.

Santa (full-body), paper mache. Beard made from bunny fur. Manufacturer unknown, N/A. 6" tall. $75-100.

Santa (face), paper mache. Beard made from bunny fur. Manufacturer unknown, 1940s. Marked US Zone Germany. 5" tall. $50-75.

Santa's bag, fabric. Manufacturer unknown, N/A. Caption: "Santa's Coal Bubble Gum." 3" tall. $3-5.

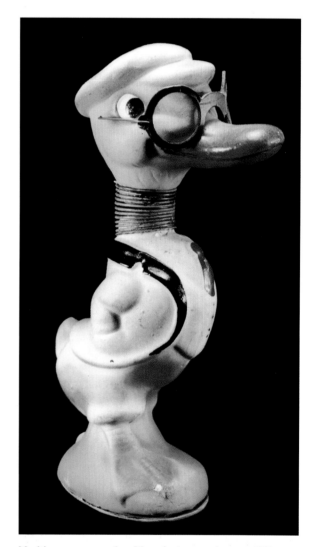

Nodder, paper mache. Manufacturer unknown, N/A. Marked Germany. A duck is wearing a pink cap and glasses. 7.5" tall. $100-150.

Nodder, paper mache. Manufacturer unknown, N/A. A Brownie is riding a rabbit. 5" tall. $500+.

Nodder, paper mache. Manufacturer unknown, N/A. Marked Germany. A duck is wearing a top hat and glasses. 8.75" tall. $100-150.

Nodder, paper mache. Manufacturer unknown, N/A. Marked Japan. A rooster is playing the accordion. 7" tall. $75-100.

Nodder, paper mache. Manufacturer unknown, N/A. Marked Japan. A rooster is standing on a green base. 7" tall. $75-100.

Rabbit, paper mache. Manufacturer unknown, N/A. A yellow rabbit wearing a brown dress. 8.5" tall. $50-75.

Nodder, paper mache. Manufacturer unknown, N/A. A duck is shown with big blue eyes. 7" tall. $75-100.

Rabbit, paper mache. Manufacturer unknown, 1940s. Marked US Zone Germany. A brown rabbit with a bag of candy tied around his neck. 2.5" tall. $40-55.

Rabbit, paper mache. Manufacturer unknown, 1940s. Marked US Zone Germany. A brown rabbit wearing a red dress and white apron. 9" tall. $50-75.

Rabbit, paper mache. Manufacturer unknown, N/A. A brown rabbit wearing a red coat and yellow pants. 7.5" tall. $75-100. **Note:** The backpack that came with the figure is not shown.

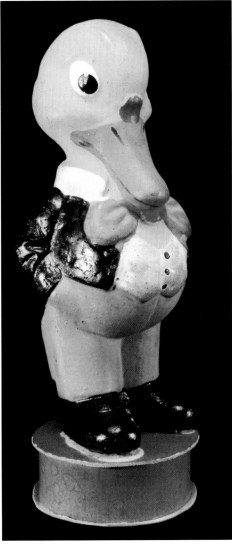

Duck, paper mache. Manufacturer unknown, N/A. A yellow duck wearing a black coat and orange pants. 7" tall. $50-75.

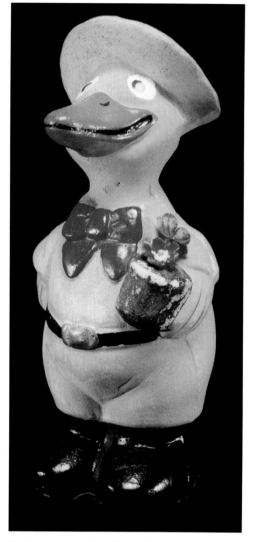

Duck, paper mache. Manufacturer unknown, N/A. A yellow duck wearing a blue hat. 6.75" tall. $40-55.

Duck, paper mache. Manufacturer unknown, N/A. A yellow duck holding a pot full of flowers. 6.75" tall. $50-75.

Bird, paper mache. Manufacturer unknown, N/A. A yellow bird wearing a top hat and orange vest. 6.25" tall. $50-75.

Duck, paper mache. Manufacturer unknown,
N/A. A yellow duck wearing a white hat and blue
cape. 6.75" tall. $50-75.

Rooster, paper mache. Manufacturer unknown,
N/A. Marked Germany. A yellow rooster standing
on a green base. 5.5" tall. $50-75.

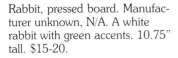

Rabbit, pressed board. Manufacturer unknown, N/A. A white
rabbit with green accents. 10.75"
tall. $15-20.

Rabbit, pressed board. Manufacturer unknown, N/A. A white rabbit with yellow accents (standing). 7.75" tall. $10-15.

Character, paper mache. Manufacturer unknown, N/A. Beard made from bunny fur. A dwarf (Bashful) wearing a gold hat and pants. 5.25" tall. $40-55.

Rabbit, pressed board. Manufacturer unknown, N/A. A white rabbit with yellow accents (laying down). 3.5" tall. $5-10.

Character, paper mache. Manufacturer unknown, N/A. Beard made from bunny fur. A dwarf (Happy) wearing a gold hat and pink pants. 4.5" tall. $40-55.

Character, paper mache. Manufacturer unknown, N/A. A dwarf (Dopey) wearing a gold hat and pants. 5.25" tall. $40-55.

Character, paper mache. Manufacturer unknown, N/A. A flying dwarf wearing a blue hat and pants. 4.5" tall. $30-45.

Character, paper mache.
Manufacturer unknown, N/A. A
dwarf (Doc) wearing a silver hat
and pants. 5.25" tall. $40-55.

Character, paper mache. Manufacturer unknown, N/A. A
dwarf (Grumpy) wearing a blue hat and pink pants. 5.25"
tall. $40-55.

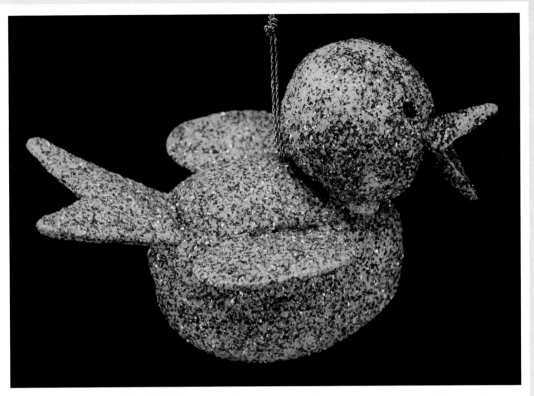

Bird, paper mache. Manufacturer unknown, N/A. A yellow bird with gold sparkles. 2.5" tall. $20-35.

Stork, paper mache with cotton. Manufacturer unknown, 1930s. Marked Germany. The wing lifts to reveal an opening. 13" tall. $250+.

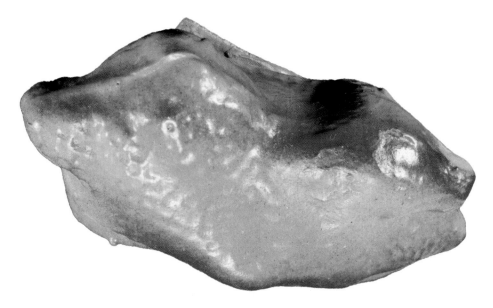

Turkey, paper mache. Manufacturer unknown, N/A. Marked Germany. 5" long. $75-100.

Valentine box, fabric. Manufacturer unknown, N/A. Box embroidered with angels. 9" tall. $20-35.

Girl, fabric. Manufacturer unknown, 1920s. Complete with purse strap. 9.25" tall. $100-150.

Chapter Four: Tin

Pail, tin. Lovell & Covel Co., N/A. Caption: "Far into the wood went Red Riding Hood." 3" tall (w/o handle). $300+.

Pail, tin. Lovell & Covel Co., N/A. Caption: "The Queen of Hearts made some tarts all on a summer's day." 3" tall (w/o handle). $300+.

Pail, tin. Lovell & Covel Co., N/A. Caption: "This little pig went to market." 3" tall (w/o handle). $300+.

Pail, tin. Lovell & Covel Co., N/A. Caption: "One look was quite enough for Peter Cottontail." 3" tall (w/o handle). $300+.

Pail, tin. Garden Co., Ltd., N/A. Children playing by the water. 2.5" tall (w/o handle). $50-75.

Pail, tin. Tindeco, N/A. Caption: "Merry Christmas from Santa." Nursery rhyme theme. 3.25" tall (w/o handle). $300+.

Pail, tin. Tindeco, N/A. Easter theme. 3.25" tall (w/o handle). $300+.

Pail, tin. Tindeco, N/A. Caption: "'Twas the night before Christmas." Santa theme. 3.25" tall (w/o handle). $300+.

Pail, tin. Tindeco, N/A. Caption: "Peter Rabbit." Easter theme. 3.25" tall (w/o handle). $300+.

Clock, tin. J.C. Crosetti Co., 1950s. Caption: "Kiddie Clock Dime Bank" 2.25" tall. $10-15. **Note:** there is a see-through enclosure on the back of the bank that reveals the candy.

Container, tin. Tindeco, N/A. Caption: "Peter Rabbit." 3.75" in diameter. $200+.

Container, tin. Henry Thorne & Co, Ltd., N/A. Marked England. Caption: "Thorne's the world's premier toffee." Kitten theme. 4" tall. $15-20.

House, tin. US Metal Toy Mfg. Co., N/A. Caption: "School P.S. 23."
The holes in the roof are to hold lollipops. 5" tall. $50-75.

House, tin. US Metal Toy Mfg. Co.,
N/A. Caption: "Merry Xmas to my
children." Santa workshop theme. The
holes in the roof are to hold lollipops.
5" tall. $50-75.

Container, tin. See's Candy Shops Inc., 1997. Caption: "See's Candies." Easter theme. 6.75" tall. $5-10.

Container, tin. Fanny Farmer Candies, 1991. Caption: "Sharing a sweet friendship." Tea party theme. Limited edition of 10,000. 7.5" tall. $10-15.

Egg, tin. J. Chein & Co., N/A. Easter bunny carrying eggs on a tray. 5.5" tall. $10-15.

Egg, tin. Manufacturer unknown, N/A. Marked Switzerland. Designed by Ian Logan. Boy riding on a train. 2.25" tall. $5-10.

Egg, tin. Manufacturer unknown, N/A. Marked Switzerland. Easter bunny carrying eggs in a boat. 2.25" tall. $5-10.

Candy/egg holder, tin. J. Chein & Co., 1950s. Chick with white wheelbarrow. 6.5" long. $50-75.

Candy/egg holder, tin. Manufacturer unknown, N/A. Rooster with blue wagon. 7.75" long. $40-55.

Candy/egg holder, tin. Wyandotte Toys, N/A. Yellow bunny in striped pants. 7.25" long. $50-75.

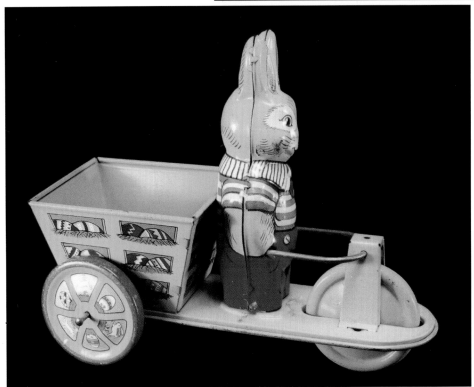

Candy/egg holder, tin. Manufacturer unknown, N/A. Brown bunny with yellow cart. 7.25" long. $40-55.

49

Candy/egg holder, tin. J. Chein & Co., 1950s. Rabbit with white wheelbarrow. 6.5" long. $50-75.

Candy/egg holder, tin. J. Chein & Co., 1950s. White rabbit with egg shaped yellow cart. 8" long. $50-75.

Candy/egg holder, tin. J. Chein & Co., N/A. Rabbit wearing red and black checkerboard pants. Nursery rhyme theme on cart. 7.5" tall. $100-150.

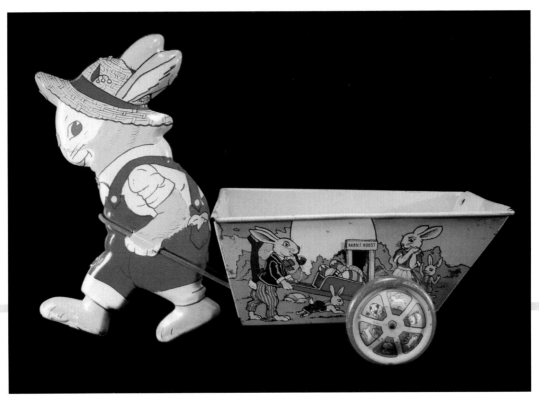

Candy/egg holder, tin. J. Chein & Co., N/A. Rabbit wearing red overalls. Caption: "Rabbit Roost." 11" long. $75-100.

Candy/egg holder, tin. J. Chein & Co., N/A. Rabbit wearing red and yellow checkerboard pants. 8.5" long. $75-100.

Candy/egg holder, tin. Wyandotte Toys, 1930s. White rabbit riding on a motorcycle. 9.25" long. $150-200.

Chapter Five: Plastic (plus)

Holiday

Rabbit, plastic. Manufacturer unknown, N/A. A yellow rabbit holding an *egg*. 5" tall. $5-10.

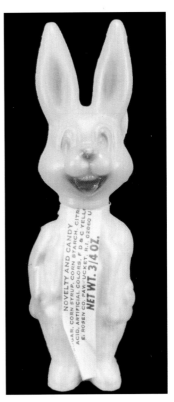

Rabbit, plastic. E. Rosen Co., N/A. A rabbit with a see-through body. 5" tall. $10-15. *Courtesy of Donna Ambeau.*

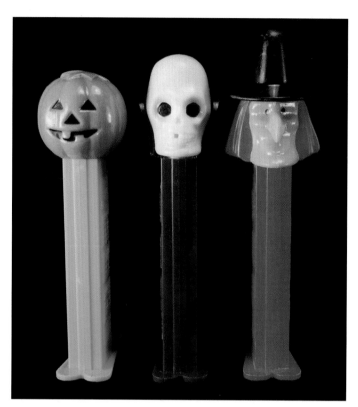

Witch, plastic. Rosbro Plastics, N/A. A witch holding
a pumpkin. 3.75" tall. $30-45.

Halloween theme, plastic. PEZ Candy Inc., 1990s. A pumpkin,
skeleton, and witch. Under 5" tall. $3-5 each.

Cat, plastic. Rosbro Plastics, N/A. A cat balancing a pumpkin. 2.75" tall. $30-45.

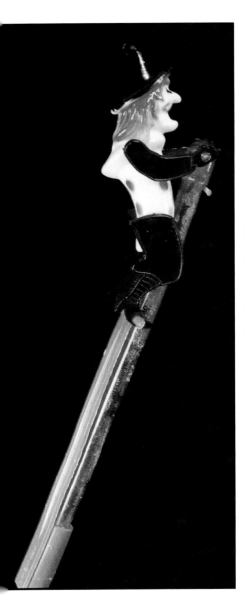

Witch, plastic. E. Rosen Co., N/A. An acrobat witch on a candy stick. 14" tall. $15-20.

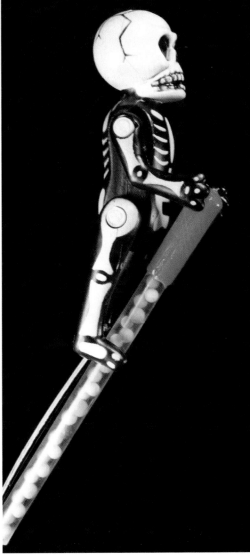

Skeleton, plastic. Bee International, N/A. An acrobat skeleton on a candy stick. 13.5" tall. $10-15.

Jack-O-Lantern, plastic. E. Rosen Co., N/A. A Jack-O-Lantern with a see-through body. 4" tall. $10-15.

Monster candy, cardboard. Four Star Candy Co., N/A. Captions: "Pottersfield. Candy Coffin Nails" and "Scar'em. Monster Size Toothpicks." 3" tall. $10-15 each.

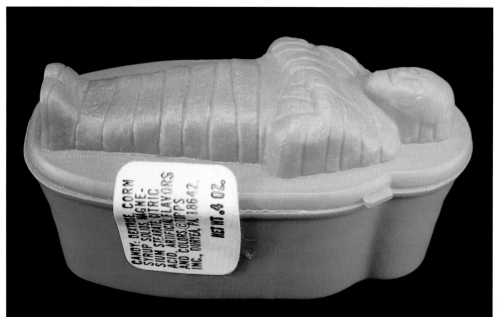

Coffin, plastic. The Topps Co., N/A. A mummy lies on top of the casket. 2.5" long. $5-10. *Courtesy of Donna Ambeau.*

Coffin (with necklace cord), plastic. Fleer Corp., N/A. Caption: "Mr. Bones." The candy is in the shape of bones that can be traded to make a full skeleton. 3" long. $5-10. *Courtesy of Donna Ambeau.*

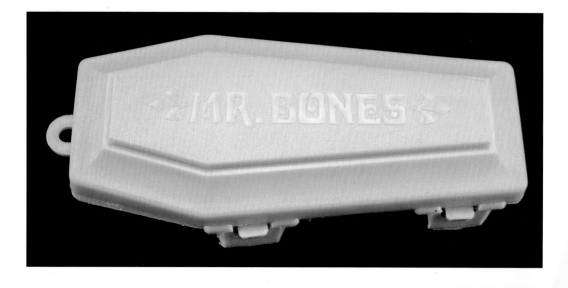

Tombstone, plastic. Leaf Confectionery, N/A. Caption: "Here lies Hank stiffer than a plank. Caught after midnight in the vault of a bank." Boot Hill Candy. 2.5" tall. $10-15. *Courtesy of Donna Ambeau.*

Tombstone, plastic. Leaf Confectionery, N/A. Caption: "Harry was a man of many faces. He died young, caught with five aces." Boot Hill Candy. 2.5" tall. $10-15. *Courtesy of Donna Ambeau.*

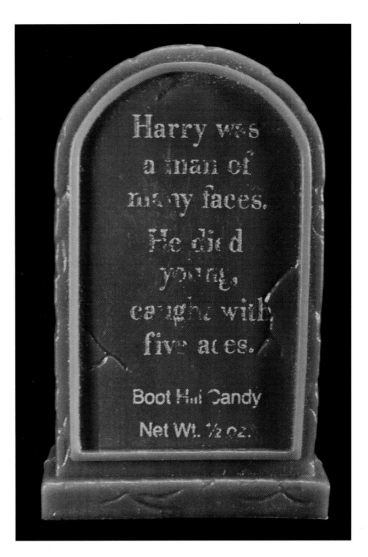

Holiday theme, plastic. PEZ Candy Inc., 1990s. A Santa, snowman, chicken, and rabbit. Under 5" tall. $1-3 each.

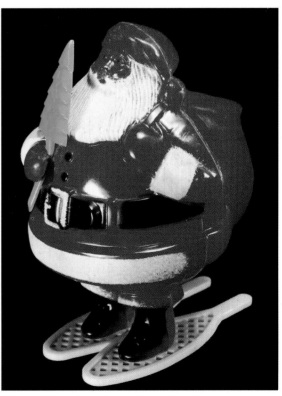

Santa, plastic. Rosbro Plastic, N/A. A Santa wearing a pair of snowshoes. 4.25" tall. $15-20.

Stocking, plastic. Rosbro Plastics, N/A. Caption: "Merry Christmas." 4" tall. $10-15.

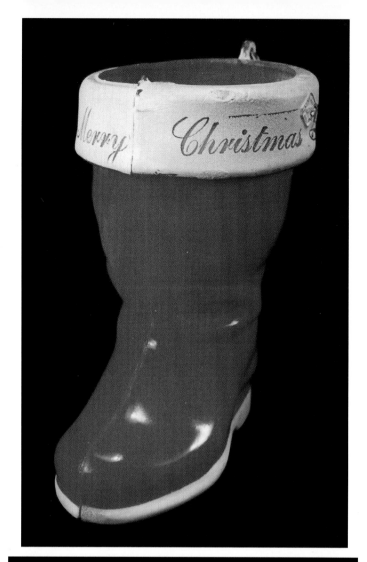

Snowman, plastic. Rosbro Plastics, N/A. A snowman smoking a pipe. 5.5" tall. $15-20.

Stocking, plastic. E. Rosen Co., N/A. Caption: "Merry Christmas." 2.5" tall. $5-10.

Food

Beverage cans, plastic. Fleer Corp., N/A. Chug-A-Can series. Caption: "Heinekant pure fun. Booed in Holland. Bail-in-time or drown in this can. Pierre's recycled mineral water." Complete with pull tab on lid. 2" tall. $15-20 each. *Courtesy of Donna Ambeau.*

Beverage cans, plastic. Fleer Corp., N/A. Crazy Can II series. Caption: "Just for Spite pour this on a friend. This is a recycled can-of-dyed water. Official military cargo A.&W.O.L. contents missing." Complete with pull tab on lid. 2" tall. $15-20 each. *Courtesy of Donna Ambeau.*

Soda, cardboard. Leaf Confectionery Inc., N/A. Caption: "Silly Soda. Dr. Preppy and Crash." 1.75" tall. $5-10 each. *Courtesy of Donna Ambeau.*

Soda, plastic. Manufacturer unknown, N/A.
Caption: "Sun-Sap Candy." 2.5" tall. $1-3.
Courtesy of Donna Ambeau.

Juice cartons, cardboard. The Topps Co., 1981. Caption: "Grape Juice.
Orange Juice." 3" tall. $1-3 each. *Courtesy of Donna Ambeau.*

Juice cartons, cardboard. The Topps Co., 1981-1984. Caption: "Pink Lemonade. Tropical Punch.
Apple Juice." 3" tall. $1-3 each. *Courtesy of Donna Ambeau.*

Shakes, plastic. Manufacturer unknown, N/A. Caption: "Sundae Shake Candy." 2.25" tall. $3-5 each. *Courtesy of Donna Ambeau.*

Pizza © Domino's Pizza Inc., cardboard. Amurol Confections Co., 1988. Caption: "Domino's Pizza Brand Bubble Gum." 2.5" tall. $15-20. *Courtesy of Donna Ambeau.*

Pizza, cardboard. Fleer Corp., N/A. Caption: "Pizza to Blo. Bubble gum with candy topping." 2.5" tall. $10-15. *Courtesy of Donna Ambeau.*

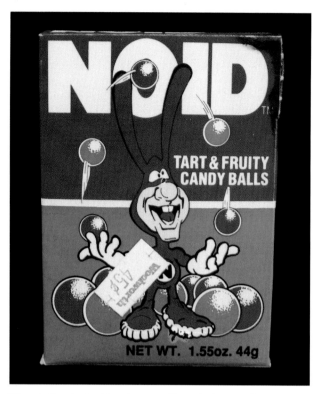

Pizza © Domino's Pizza Inc., cardboard. Amurol Confections Co., 1988. Caption: "NOID created in Claymation by Will Vinton." 3.25" tall. $15-20. *Courtesy of Donna Ambeau.*

Chinese food, cardboard. The Topps Co., 1985. Caption: "Chew Fun Bubble Gum Noodles." 2.5" tall (w/ handle). $15-20. *Courtesy of Donna Ambeau.*

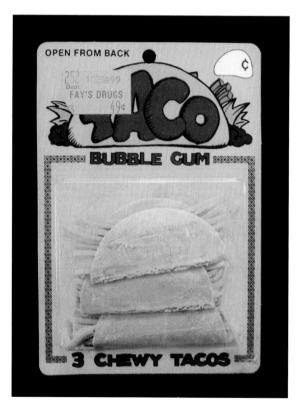

Taco, candy. Amurol Confections Co., N/A. Caption: "3 Chewy Tacos. Bubble Gum." 5.75" tall. $3-5. *Courtesy of Donna Ambeau.*

Chinese food, cardboard. R.M. Palmer Co., 2001. Caption: "Fortune Hearts." 4.4" tall (w/ handle) $3-5.

Hot dog, cardboard. Philadelphia Chewing Gum Corp./Swell Confections, Ltd., N/A. Caption: "Looks like a hot dog... tastes like gum. Doggie Man – Hey... Getcha Hot Dog." 4.25" long. $3-5. *Courtesy of Donna Ambeau.*

Hot dog, plastic wrap. Leaf Confectionery Inc., N/A. "Hot Dog! Bubble Gum." Contains 10 hot dog-shaped bubble gum pieces. 2.75" tall. $1-3. *Courtesy of Donna Ambeau.*

TV Dinner, plastic. Fleer Corp., N/A. Crazy TV dinner series. Caption: "Windy's Dinner. Crazy TV Dinner #20." 1.75" tall. $15-20. *Courtesy of Donna Ambeau.*

Hamburger, foil wrap. Fleer Corp., N/A. Caption: "Where's the Beef?" Wendy's restaurant promotion. 1.75" in diameter. $10-15. *Courtesy of Donna Ambeau.*

French fries, cardboard. Leaf Confectionery Inc., N/A. Caption: "French Fry Bubble Gum." Contains 7 French fry-shaped pieces of gum. 3.25" tall. $3-5. *Courtesy of Donna Ambeau.*

Hamburger, plastic. Fleer Corp., N/A. Caption: "Bubble Burger 100% Pure Bubble Gum." 2" tall. $3-5. *Courtesy of Donna Ambeau.*

Hamburger, plastic wrap.
Timberline Industries II, Inc.,
N/A. Caption: "Burger Gummi
Candy." 1.5" tall. $1-3. *Courtesy
of Donna Ambeau.*

Ice cream cone, plastic, The
Topps Co., 1982. 2.25" tall.
$5-10. *Courtesy of Donna
Ambeau.*

Ice cream cone, plastic. Manufacturer unknown,
1996. 3" tall. $3-5.

Pickle (with necklace cord),
plastic. Creative Confection
Concepts, Inc., N/A. Caption:
"Pickle Puss." 5.5" tall. $5-10.
Courtesy of Donna Ambeau.

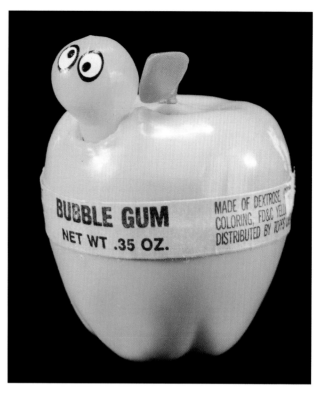

Apple, plastic. The Topps Co., N/A. Green apple with a yellow worm. 2.25" tall. $5-10. *Courtesy of Donna Ambeau.*

Pickle (with necklace cord), plastic. Creative Confection Concepts Inc., N/A. Caption: "Piccolo Bubble Gum." 3.25" tall. $5-10. *Courtesy of Donna Ambeau.*

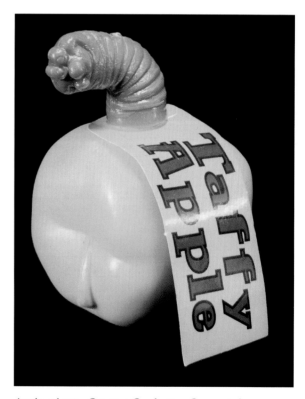

Apple, plastic. Creative Confection Concepts Inc., 1990s. Caption: "Taffy Apple." 2.75" tall. $5-10. *Courtesy of Donna Ambeau.*

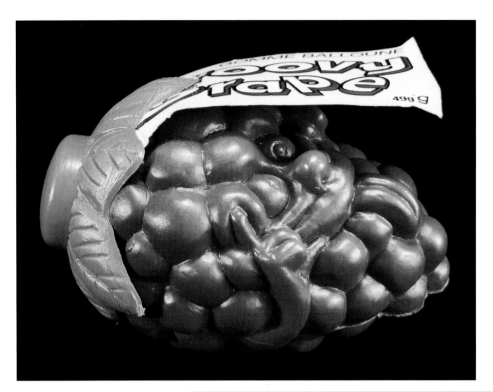

Grape, plastic. Creative Confections Concepts Inc., N/A. Caption: "Groovy Grape." 4" tall. $5-10. *Courtesy of Donna Ambeau.*

Watermelon, cardboard. Willy Wonka Brands, N/A. Caption: "Watermelon Giant Seedless Candy Jawbreakers." 1.5" tall. $10-15. *Courtesy of Donna Ambeau.*

Berries, plastic. Leaf Confectionery Inc., N/A. Caption: "Raspberry and Strawberry Bubble Gum." 1.75" tall. $3-5 each. *Courtesy of Donna Ambeau.*

Eggs, plastic. Leaf Confectionary Inc., N/A. Caption: "Eggums." Contains 12 pieces of bubble gum eggs. 3.75" long. $5-10. *Courtesy of Donna Ambeau.*

Cereal box, cardboard. Fun Foods Inc., N/A. Zilly-Zereal series. Caption: "General Ma. Loco Ruffs. 3" tall. $15-20. *Courtesy of Donna Ambeau.*

Egg cartons, cardboard. Pacific Promotions Hawaii, N/A. Caption: "Gecko Eggs." South Cape Distributors, Inc., N/A. Caption: "Lobster eggs." 3" tall. $3-5 each. *Courtesy of Donna Ambeau.*

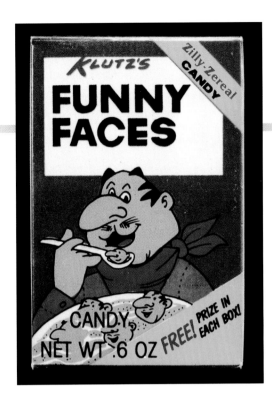

Cereal box, cardboard. Fun Foods Inc., N/A. Zilly-Zereal series. Caption: "Klutz's Funny Faces." 3" tall. $15-20. *Courtesy of Donna Ambeau.*

Pumpkin, foil wrap. Fleer Corp., N/A. Caption: "Giant Pumpkin Face Bubble Gum. Crack it like a candy… chew it like a gum." 4.5" tall. $10-15. *Courtesy of Donna Ambeau.*

Cereal box, cardboard. Fun Foods Inc., N/A. Zilly-Zereal series. Caption: "Klutz's Nice Kreapies." 3" tall. $15-20. *Courtesy of Donna Ambeau.*

Household Items

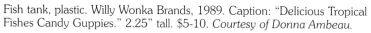

Fish tank, plastic. Willy Wonka Brands, 1989. Caption: "Delicious Tropical Fishes Candy Guppies." 2.25" tall. $5-10. *Courtesy of Donna Ambeau.*

Aquarium, plastic. Amurol Confections Co., 1995. Caption: "Squeeze-Pop Aquarium Candy Blue Raspberry." 5.5" long. $10-15. *Courtesy of Donna Ambeau.*

Mailbox, plastic. Fleer Corp., N/A.
2.75" tall. $5-10. *Courtesy of Donna Ambeau.*

Combat bag, paper. Donruss Co., N/A. Caption: "Combat Rations." 2.75" tall. $10-15. *Courtesy of Donna Ambeau.*

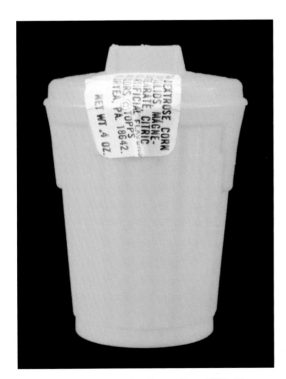

Garbage can, plastic. The Topps Co., 1990. The candy is in the shape of garbage (i.e., fish bones). 2" tall. $5-10. *Courtesy of Donna Ambeau.*

Garbage bag, plastic. The Topps Co., 1986. Caption: "Garbage Pail Kids Cheap Toy with Candy." 3.75" tall. $10-15. *Courtesy of Donna Ambeau.*

Sports bottle, plastic. Amurol Confections Co., 1992. Caption: "Squeeze-Pop Sports Bottle." 5.25" tall. $3-5. *Courtesy of Donna Ambeau.*

Recycle bin, plastic. Leaf Confectionery Inc., 1994. Caption: "Re-Use-It Righteously Recycled Bubble Gum." 1.75" tall. $5-10. *Courtesy of Donna Ambeau.*

Baby bottle, plastic. The Topps Co., N/A. Caption: "Baby Bottle Pop Candy." 3.75" tall. $1-3. *Courtesy of Donna Ambeau.*

Jug, plastic. Amurol Confections Co., N/A. Caption: "Shake n' Chug. Tropical Fruit Bubble Jug." 3.5" tall. $1-3. *Courtesy of Donna Ambeau.*

Right:
Baby bottle, plastic. Albert & Sons Inc., N/A. Caption: "Will You Be My Big Baby." 4.24" tall. $1-3.

Bug jar, plastic. Amurol Confections Co., 1992. Caption: "Bug City Candy Tarts. Re-usable bug jar." 2.75" tall. $1-3. *Courtesy of Donna Ambeau.*

Cooler, plastic. Color Fun Foods Inc., N/A. Caption: "Playmate." The candy is in the shape of soda cans. 2" tall. $5-10. *Courtesy of Donna Ambeau.*

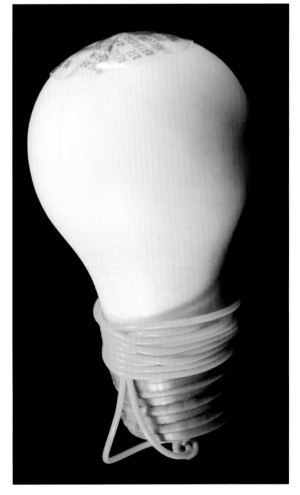

Lunchbox, plastic. The Topps Co., N/A. 2" tall. $5-10. *Courtesy of Donna Ambeau.*

Light bulb (with necklace cord), plastic. The Topps Co., 1981. 2.5" tall. $5-10. *Courtesy of Donna Ambeau.*

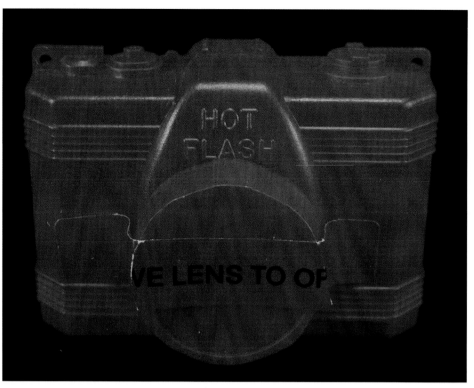

Lava lamp © Haggerty Enterprises, Inc., plastic. Amurol Confections Co., 1994. Caption: "Squeeze-Pop Lava Lick Liquid Candy." $3-5. *Courtesy of Donna Ambeau.*

Camera, plastic. Donruss Co., N/A. Caption: "Hot Flash." 1.75" tall. $5-10. *Courtesy of Donna Ambeau.*

Checkbook, vinyl. Amurol Confections Co., 1994. Caption: "Checkbook Bubble Gum." The bubble gum checks are printed with payees like: "Pig E. Bank" and "Bo Gus Bucks." 5.75" long. $1-3. *Courtesy of Donna Ambeau.*

Film, foil wrap. Candy Corp., N/A. Caption: "Today Mini-Milk Chocolate Film. Film Type 48." 1.5" tall. $10-15. *Courtesy of Donna Ambeau.*

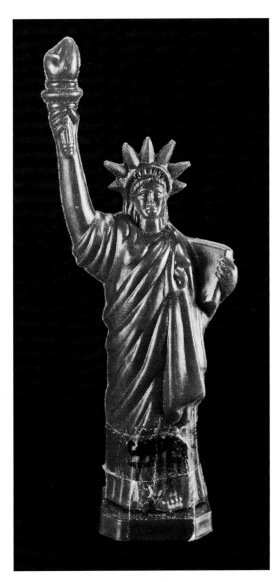

Gumball machine (with key chain), plastic. Hilco Corp., N/A. Candy is dispensed when the front button is pressed. 3.75" tall. $1-3. *Courtesy of Donna Ambeau.*

Statue of Liberty, plastic. The Topps Co., 1986. 4.75" tall. $5-10. *Courtesy of Donna Ambeau.*

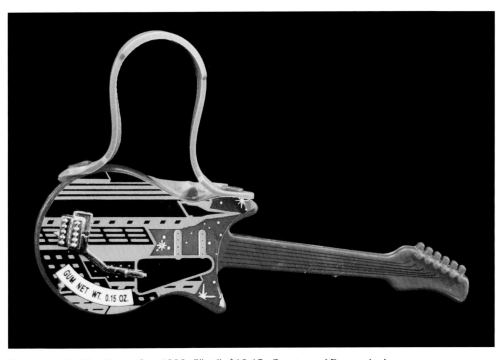

Guitar, plastic. The Topps Co., 1992. 5" tall. $10-15. *Courtesy of Donna Ambeau.*

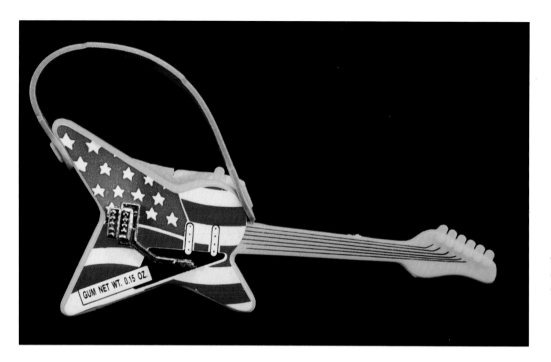

V-shaped Guitar, plastic. The Topps Company, 1992. 5" tall. $10-15. *Courtesy of Donna Ambeau.*

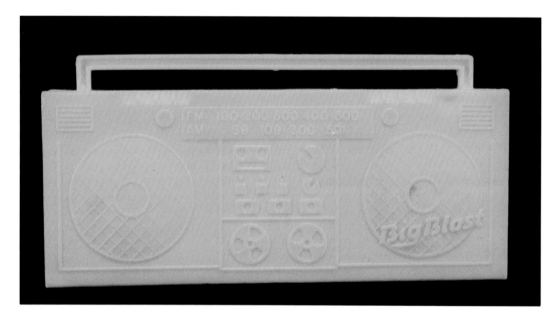

Radio, plastic. Fleer Corp., 1984. Caption: "Big Blast Radio." 1.5" tall. $5-10. *Courtesy of Donna Ambeau.*

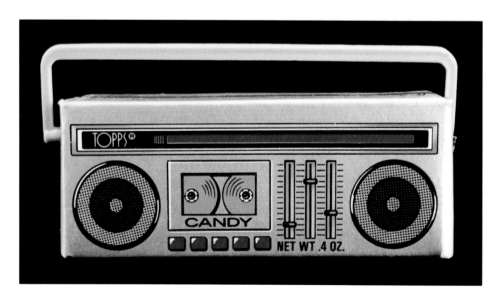

Radio, cardboard. The Topps Co., 1986. Caption: "Boom Box Candy." 1.5" tall (with handle). $10-15. *Courtesy of Donna Ambeau.*

Record, cardboard. Amurol Confections Co., 1980s. Chu-Bops Gold Album Collection. Caption: "Elvis Presley." Limited edition. The gum is in the shape of a record. 3" tall. $10-15. *Courtesy of Donna Ambeau.*

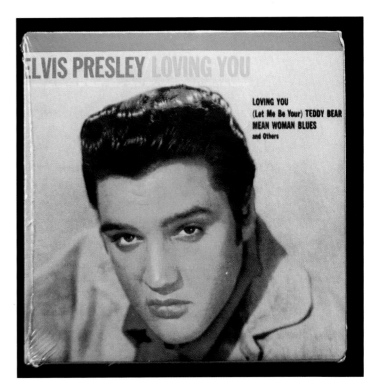

Record, cardboard. Amurol Confections Co., 1980s. Chu-Bops Gold Album Collection. Caption: "Elvis Presley. Loving You." Limited edition. The gum is in the shape of a record. 3" tall. $10-15. *Courtesy of Donna Ambeau.*

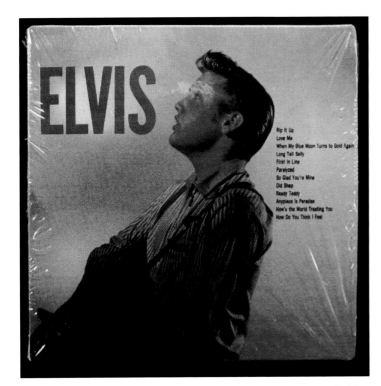

Record, cardboard. Amurol Confections Co., 1980s. Chu-Bops Gold Album Collection. Caption: "Elvis." Limited edition. The gum is in the shape of a record. 3" tall. $10-15. *Courtesy of Donna Ambeau.*

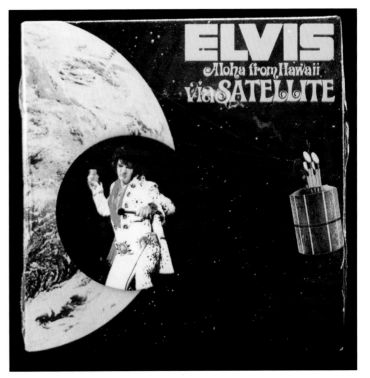

Record, cardboard. Amurol Confections Co., 1980s. Chu-Bops Gold Album Collection series. Caption: "Elvis. Aloha from Hawaii via Satellite." Limited edition. The gum is in the shape of a record. 3" tall. $10-15. *Courtesy of Donna Ambeau.*

Record, cardboard. Amurol Confections Co., 1980s. Superstar Chu-Bops Miniature Album Collection #50. Caption: "Journey. Escape." The gum is in the shape of a record. 3" tall. $10-15.

Record, cardboard. Amurol Confections Co., 1980s. Chu-Bops Miniature Album Collection #5. Caption: "Get the Knack." The gum is in the shape of a record. 3" tall. $10-15.

Record, cardboard. Amurol Confections Co., 1980s. Chu-Bops Miniature Album Collection #9. Caption: "Blondie. Parallel Lines." The gum is in the shape of a record. 3" tall. $10-15.

Record, cardboard. Amurol Confections Co., 1980s. Chu-Bops Miniature Album Collection #4. Caption: "Billy Joel. Glass Houses." The gum is in the shape of a record. 3" tall. $10-15.

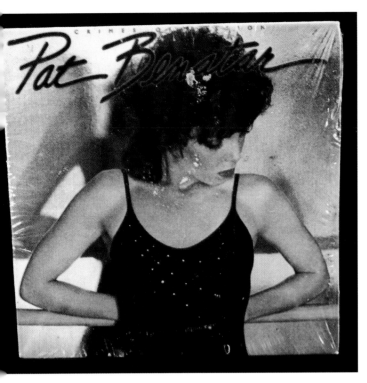

Record, cardboard. Amurol Confections Co., 1980s. Chu-Bops Miniature Album Collection #25. Caption: "Pat Benatar. Crimes of Passion." The gum is in the shape of a record. 3" tall. $10-15.

Record, cardboard. Amurol Confections Co., 1980s. Chu-Bops Miniature Album Collection #37. Caption: "Rush. Moving Pictures." The gum is in the shape of a record. 3" tall. $10-15.

Compact disc, plastic/paper. Zeebs Enterprises Inc., N/A. CD's Digital Gum Series. Caption: "Saltin' Pepomint." Songs include: "1) Bubblz 'n the 'Hood. 2) Pop! There It Is. 3) My Bubbles on Broadway. 4) Doin' da Bubble. 5) Bloomp Bloomp a Bloomp. 6) Hip Pop Groove 7) How Blow Can You Go? 8) Cold chewin'." The gum is in the shape of a CD. 5" tall. $10-15. *Courtesy of Donna Ambeau.*

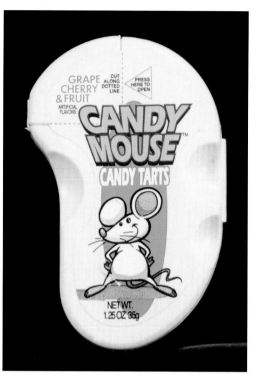

Compact disc, plastic/paper. Zeebs Enterprises Inc., N/A. CD's Digital Gum Series. Caption: "ZZ Pop Afterburst." Songs include: "1) Gimmie All Your Bubblin'. 2) Sharp Dressed Gum. 3) She's Got Sticks (and She Knows How to Chew 'Em). 4) Bubbles Under Pressure. 5) Sleeping Bubble. 5) Chew Gum Classes." The gum is in the shape of a CD. 5" tall. $10-15. *Courtesy of Donna Ambeau.*

Computer mouse, plastic. Amurol Confections Co., N/A. Caption: "Candy Mouse Candy Tarts." 3.75" tall (without tail). $3-5. *Courtesy of Donna Ambeau.*

Cassette tape, plastic/paper. The Topps Co., 1989. Caption: "The Living Dead Live. Home of the Grave. Gory Days. My Brother's a Stiff." 3" tall. $10-15. *Courtesy of Donna Ambeau.*

Telephone, plastic. R.L. Albert & Sons Inc., N/A. Caption: "Hello Candy." 1.5" tall. $15-20.

Pay phone, plastic. Fleer Corp., N/A. Caption: "Phoney Candy." The candy is in the shape of coins. 2.75" tall. $5-10. *Courtesy of Donna Ambeau.*

Beeper, plastic. Amurol Confections Co., N/A. Caption: "Bubble Beeper." Contains 17 sticks of gum. 3.25" tall. $3-5. *Courtesy of Donna Ambeau.*

Dog house, plastic. Fleer Corp., N/A. Caption: "Dawg House." The candy is in the shape of a hot dog. 2.75" long. $5-10. *Courtesy of Donna Ambeau.*

Cellular phone, plastic. Amurol Confections Co., N/A. Caption: "Cellular Bubble Gum." 6.25" tall. $3-5. *Courtesy of Donna Ambeau.*

Fire hydrant, plastic. Fleer Corp., N/A. 2.75" tall. $5-10. *Courtesy of Donna Ambeau.*

Cigarettes, cardboard. World Candies Inc., N/A. Captions: "Lucky Lights" and "Kings." 3.25" tall. $10-15 each.

Cigars, gum/paper label. Philadelphia Chewing Gum Corp., 1988. Caption: "The Duke in '88. Win with Bush." 5.75" long. $3-5 each. *Courtesy of Donna Ambeau.*

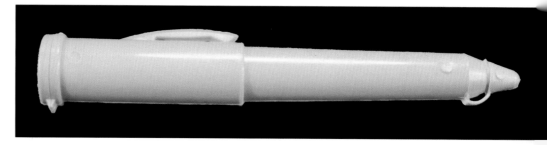

Pen, plastic. The Topps Co., N/A. The tip of the pen opens to dispense candy. 5.25" tall. $5-10. *Courtesy of Donna Ambeau.*

Crayons, cardboard. Philadelphia Chewing Gum Corp., N/A. Caption: "Chewola Bubble Gum. A Time to Love." 4" tall. $3-5. *Courtesy of Donna Ambeau.*

Notebook, cardboard. The Topps Co., 1986. Caption: "Sneaky Snacks." 3" tall. $10-15. *Courtesy of Donna Ambeau.*

Crayon, plastic. Philadelphia Chewing Gum Corp., N/A. Caption: "Crayon Fruit Pop." 3.75" tall. $1-3. *Courtesy of Donna Ambeau.*

Notebook, plastic. Fleer Corp., N/A. Caption: "Give Me a Hug." 2.25" tall. $5-10.

Lipstick, plastic. The Topps Co., 1985. Caption: "Push Pop. Grape and Cherry." 3" tall. $1-3 each. *Courtesy of Donna Ambeau.*

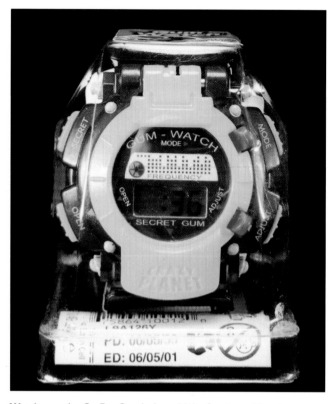

Watch, candy. Ce De Candy Inc., N/A. Caption: "Candy Watch." 3" tall. $5-10.

Band-aids, tin. Amurol Confections Co., N/A. Caption: "Ouch! Bubble Gum." Contains 21 sticks of gum. 3.5" tall. $1-3 each. *Courtesy of Donna Ambeau.*

Spray cans, plastic. Fleer, Corp., N/A. Crazy Spray Can Series. Caption: "Add Skunk Spray to your classroom – and leave school early! Spray-on Onion Spray Fast Cry Baby Action. Mit-Gum Spray Mess Super Stick All Day Formula." 2.5" tall. $15-20 each. *Courtesy of Donna Ambeau.*

Paint can, tin. Concord Confections, Inc., N/A. Caption: "Tongue Splashers Bubble Gum." Contains 15 pieces of gum. 2" tall. $1-3. *Courtesy of Donna Ambeau.*

Paint roller, plastic. The Topps Co., 1994. Caption: "Roller Pop Candy. Candy n' Powder that Paints Your Mouth." 4.5" tall. $3-5. *Courtesy of Donna Ambeau.*

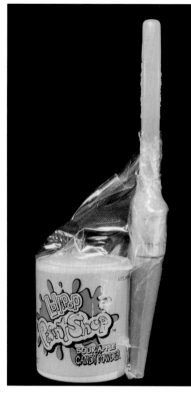

Paint and brush, candy/plastic. Impact Confections Inc., N/A. Caption: "Lollipop Paint Shop. Sour Apple Candy Powder." 6.5" tall. $1-3. *Courtesy of Donna Ambeau.*

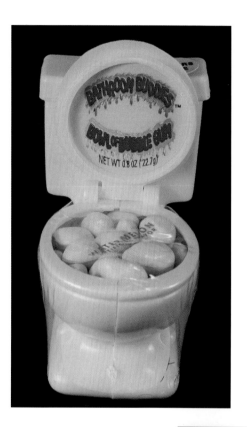

Toilet, plastic. The Topps Co., 1996. Caption: "Bathroom Buddies. Bowl of Bubble Gum." 3" tall. $5-10.

Slot machine, plastic. Amurol Confections Co., 1995. Caption: "Bubble Jackpot Bubble Gum." 3.75" tall. $5-10. *Courtesy of Donna Ambeau.*

Fly, plastic/rubber. The Topps Co., 1992. The fly's stomach contains gum. Complete with suction cup. 1.5" tall. $5-10. *Courtesy of Donna Ambeau.*

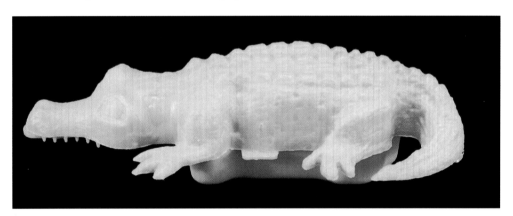

Alligator, plastic. Philadelphia Chewing Gum Corp., N/A. 3.75" long. $5-10. *Courtesy of Donna Ambeau.*

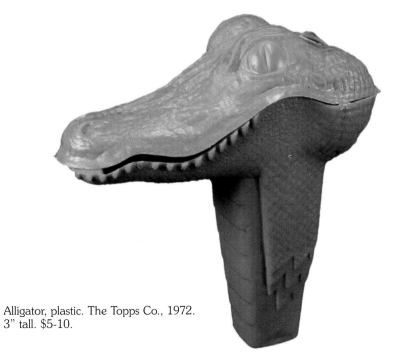

Alligator, plastic. The Topps Co., 1972. 3" tall. $5-10.

Snakes, plastic wrap. Trolli Inc./Mederer, N/A. Caption: "Gummi Snakes in the Grass." 3.25" in diameter. $1-3. *Courtesy of Donna Ambeau.*

Ants, plastic wrap. Fleer Corp, 1988. Caption: "Sand Hill Bubble Gum that Pours with Candy Ants." 3" tall. $10-15. *Courtesy of Donna Ambeau.*

Vehicles

Truck, plastic. Imperial Toy Corp./ Willy Wonka Brands, 1995. Caption: "Candy Express." 7" long. $5-10. *Courtesy of Donna Ambeau.*

Car, plastic. Manufacturer unknown, N/A. Complete with straw. 1.25" tall. $3-5. *Courtesy of Donna Ambeau.*

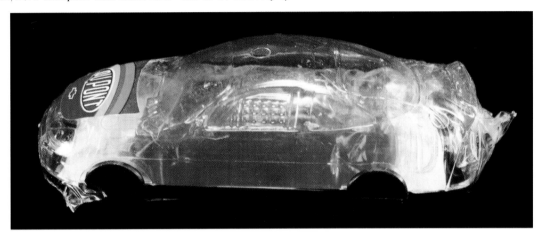

Car, plastic. High Performance Sports Marketing, N/A. Caption: "Dupont." 4.5" long. $3-5.
Courtesy of Donna Ambeau.

Car, plastic. Zeebs Enterprises, N/A. Caption: "Gummi Karz. Huge Gummi & Decals Inside." 4.5" long.
$3-5. *Courtesy of Donna Ambeau.*

Left:
Locker, plastic. Fleer Corp., N/A. The candy is in the shape of books and socks. 3.25" tall. $5-10. *Courtesy of Donna Ambeau.*

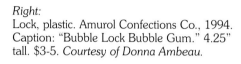

Right:
Lock, plastic. Amurol Confections Co., 1994. Caption: "Bubble Lock Bubble Gum." 4.25" tall. $3-5. *Courtesy of Donna Ambeau.*

Locker, tin. Amurol Confections Co., N/A. Caption: "Bubble Locker." 3.25" tall. $1-3. *Courtesy of Donna Ambeau.*

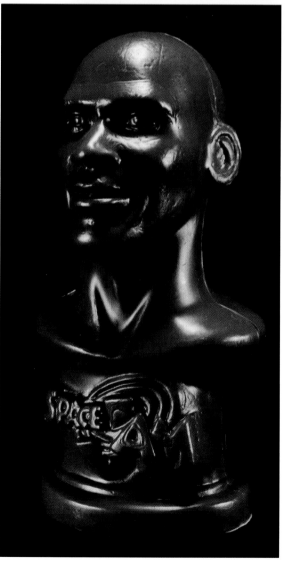

Michael Jordan / Space Jam © Warner Bros., plastic. Creative Confection Concepts Inc., 1996. Caption: "Trophy Treats. Basketball Gumballs!" 5.25" tall. $15-20. *Courtesy of Donna Ambeau.*

Sneakers, cardboard. Berzerk Candy Werks/Division of KFI Corp., N/A. Caption: "Air Gummi. Candy High Tops." 3.25" long. $15-20. *Courtesy of Donna Ambeau.*

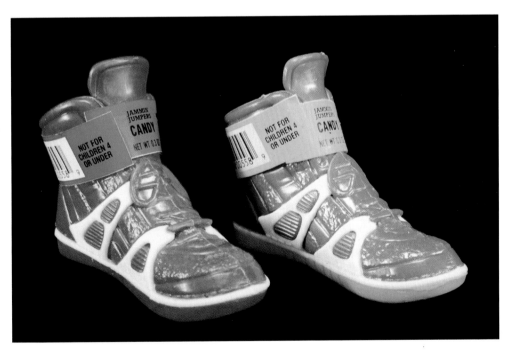

Sneakers, cardboard. The Topps Co., 1990. Jammin' Jumpers series. 2.25" tall. $5-10 each. *Courtesy of Donna Ambeau.*

Roller skate (with necklace cord), plastic. Topps Chewing Gum Inc., 1980s. Moveable wheels. 2.25" tall. $5-10. *Courtesy of Donna Ambeau.*

Rollerblade, plastic. The Topps Co., 1990s. Moveable wheels. 3" tall. $10-15. *Courtesy of Donna Ambeau.*

Dumbbell, plastic. Frankford Candy & Chocolate, Co., N/A. Caption: "Gum-Bell Dumb-Bell." 6.5" long. $3-5. *Courtesy of Donna Ambeau.*

Football, plastic. Fleer Corp., N/A. Caption: "Game Time." 2" tall. $5-10.

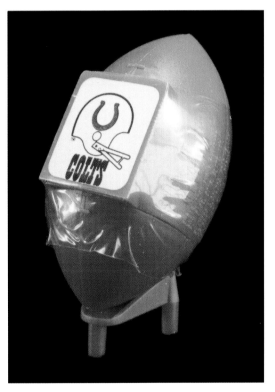

Football, plastic. Donruss, Co., N/A. Caption: "Colts." 3.25" tall. $5-10. *Courtesy of Donna Ambeau.*

Tennis balls, plastic/cardboard. Donruss Co., N/A. Caption: "Don't Flop. Designed especially for big time bubble blowing." Contains 3 pieces of gum in the shape of tennis balls. 3" tall. $15-20. *Courtesy of Donna Ambeau.*

Golf balls, gum/cardboard. Leaf Confectionery Inc., N/A. Caption: "Golf Ball Bubble Gum for long chewing big bubbles." Contains 3 pieces of gum in the shape of golf balls. 3.5" tall. $10-15. *Courtesy of Donna Ambeau.*

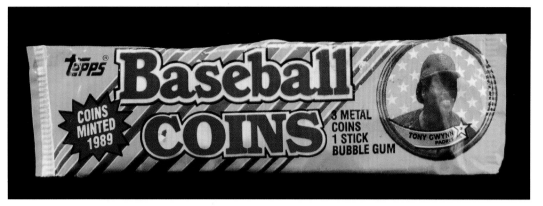

Baseball coins, plastic wrap. The Topps Co., 1989. Caption: "Baseball Coins. Tony Gwynn of the Padres. Three metal coins." Contains one stick bubble gum. 5.75" long. $10-15. *Courtesy of Donna Ambeau.*

Boy in baseball uniform, plastic. E. Rosen Co., N/A. 5.75" tall. $5-10. *Courtesy of Donna Ambeau.*

Body Parts

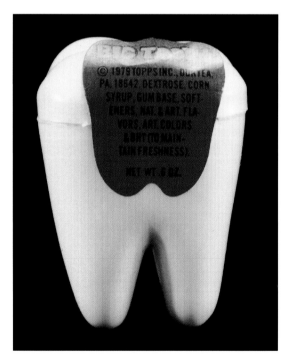

Tooth, plastic. The Topps Co., 1979. Caption: "Big Tooth." 2.25" tall. $5-10. *Courtesy of Donna Ambeau.*

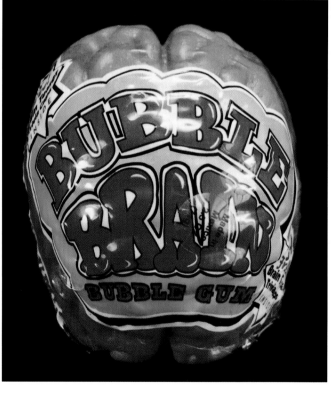

Brain, plastic. Creative Confection Concepts Inc., N/A. Caption: "Bubble Brain Bubble Gum. Five free brain teaser trivia caps inside." 2.5" tall. $5-10. *Courtesy of Donna Ambeau.*

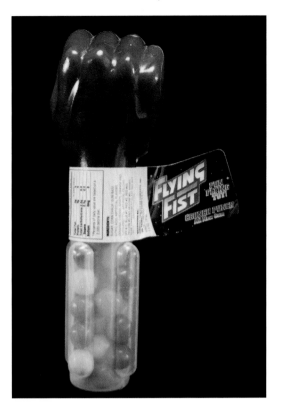

Fist, plastic. Creative Confection Concepts Inc., N/A. Caption: "Flying Fist. Fun Flying Toy! Crunch Punch All New Gum." 6.25" tall. $3-5. *Courtesy of Donna Ambeau.*

Brain, plastic. OddzOn Inc., 1999. Caption: "No Brainer Pop." 5.25" tall. $3-5.

Boogers, plastic wrap. Confex Inc., N/A. Caption: "Boogers Gummy Candy." 3.25" tall. $10-15. *Courtesy of Donna Ambeau.*

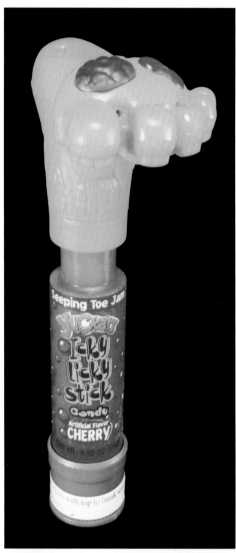

Foot, plastic. OddzOn Inc., 2000. Caption: "Seeping Toe Jam Yuckers Icky Licky Stick Candy." 6.5" tall. $3-5.

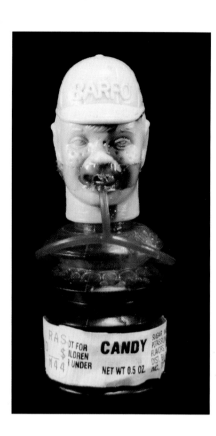

Barfo, plastic. The Topps Co., 1989. 3.25" tall. $10-15. *Courtesy of Donna Ambeau.* **Note:** A "Barfo" mom, dad, and dog were also made.

Space and Robot

Alien UFO, cardboard. The Foreign Candy Co., 1997. Caption: "Alien UFO spaceships Candy Wafers." 6.5" tall. $10-15. *Courtesy of Donna Ambeau.*

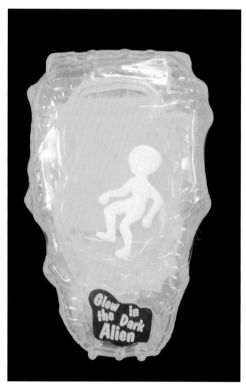

Alien, plastic. R.L. Albert & Son Inc., N/A. Caption: "Glow in the Dark Alien." 4" tall. $5-10. *Courtesy of Donna Ambeau.*

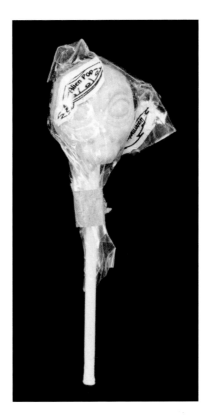

Alien lollipop. Impact Confections Inc., N/A. Caption: "Alien Pop." 4.75" tall. $1-3. *Courtesy of Donna Ambeau.*

Space taste, plastic. Uniconfis Corporation, N/A. Caption: "Space Taste Squeezable Candy." 3.5" tall. $10-15. *Courtesy of Donna Ambeau.*

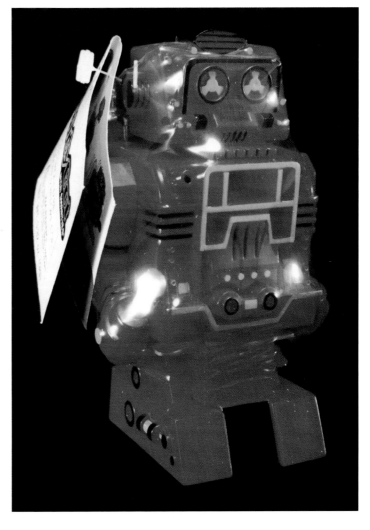

Space worms, plastic wrap. Glenn Candies, N/A. Caption: "Space Worms. Blue Raspberry and Cherry Filled with Space Powder." 5.75" tall. $10-15. *Courtesy of Donna Ambeau.*

Robot, plastic. Perfect Candy Co./Busy Kids Inc., 1999. 5" tall. $5-10.

Addams Family © Hanna-Barbera (Gomez),
plastic. Bee International, 1993. 4.5" tall. $5-10.

Addams Family © Hanna-Barbera (Lurch), plastic.
Bee International, 1993. 4.5" tall. $5-10.

Alf © Alien Productions, plastic. The Topps Co., 1987. 2.5" tall. $15-20. *Courtesy of Donna Ambeau.*

Addams Family © Hanna-Barbera (Uncle Fester), plastic. Bee International, 1993. 4" tall. $5-10.

Below:
Animaniacs © Warner Bros., plastic. The Topps Co., 1995. Caption: "Wakko, Yakko, and Dot." 2.75" tall. $5-10 each. *Courtesy of Donna Ambeau.*

Bingo © Tri-Star Pictures, Inc., plastic. The Topps Co., 1991. Bingo's dog dish. 2.25" in diameter. $5-10. *Courtesy of Donna Ambeau.*

Batman (and friends) © DC & Marvel Comics, plastic. PEZ Candy Inc., c. 1990s. Batman, Spiderman, The Incredible Hulk, and Wonder Woman. Under 5" tall. $3-5 each.

Batman © DC Comics, plastic. The Topps Co., 1989. 2.75" tall. $5-10 each. *Courtesy of Donna Ambeau.*

Batman © DC Comics. The Topps Co., 1989. 2.5" tall. $5-10.

Batman character (The Joker) © DC Comics, plastic. The Topps Co., 1989. 2.5" tall. $5-10.

Batmobile © DC Comics, plastic. The Topps Co., 1991. 3.75" long. $10-15. *Courtesy of Donna Ambeau.*

Batman character (The Riddler) © DC Comics, plastic. The Topps Co., 1995. 2.5" tall. $5-10.

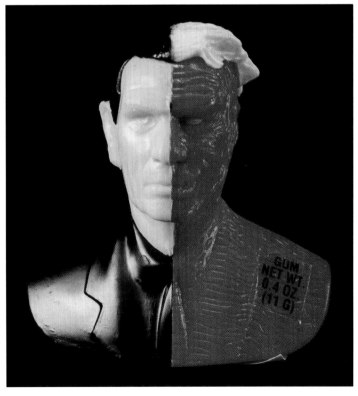

Batman character (Two Face) © DC Comics, plastic. The Topps Co., 1995. 2.25" tall. $5-10.

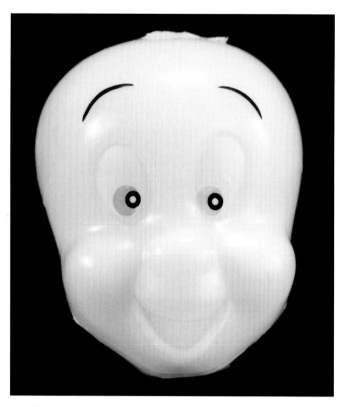

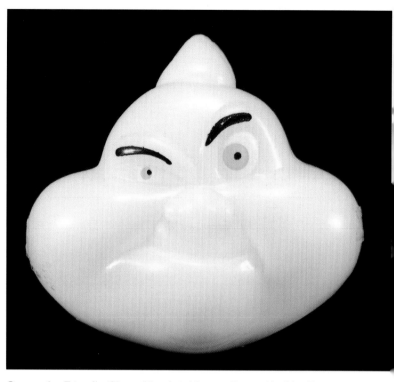

Casper the Friendly Ghost (Casper) © Harvey Comics/ Amblin Entertainment, Inc., plastic. The Topps Co., 1995. 2.25" tall. $5-10. *Courtesy of Donna Ambeau.*

Casper the Friendly Ghost (Fatso) © Harvey Comics/Amblin Entertainment, Inc., plastic. The Topps Co., 1995. 2.25" tall. $5-10.

Dick Tracy © The Walt Disney Company, plastic. The Topps Co., 1990. Captions: "Big Boy and Rodent Candy." 2.5" tall. $5-10 each. *Courtesy of Donna Ambeau.*

Casper the Friendly Ghost (Stretch) © Harvey Comics/Amblin Entertainment, Inc., plastic. The Topps Co., 1995. 2.25" tall. $5-10.

Catdog © Peter Hannan/Viacom International Inc., vinyl. Amurol Confections Co., 1999. 7.25" long. $3-5.

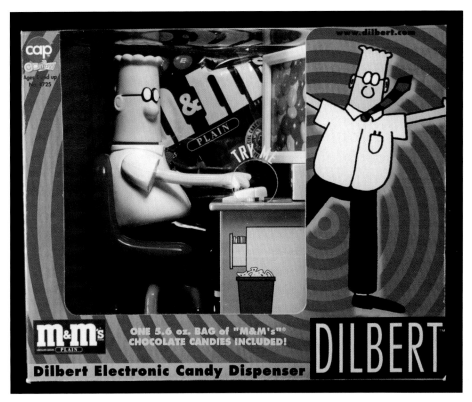

Dilbert © Scott Adams/UFS, plastic. OddzOn Inc., 1998. Caption: "Dilbert Electronic Candy Dispenser." 7" tall. $15-20.

Dilbert © Scott Adams/UFS, tin. Ragold Inc., 2001. Captions: "Invest-mints" and "Harrass-mints." 2.5" tall. $1-3.

Dilbert © Scott Adams/UFS, tin. Ragold Inc., 2001. Captions: "Empower-mints" and "Postpone-mints." 2.5" tall. $1-3.

Donald Duck (and friends) © Walt Disney Company, plastic. PEZ Candy Inc., 1990s. Donald Duck, Daisy Duck, Minnie Mouse, and Mickey Mouse. Under 5" tall. $3-5 each.

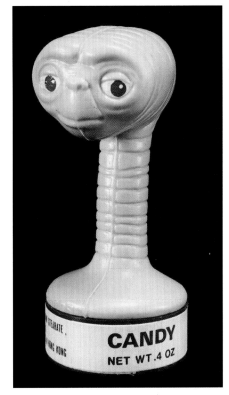

E.T. © Universal Studios, plastic. The
Topps Co., 1982. 2.75" tall. $15-20.
Courtesy of Donna Ambeau.

The Flintstones © Hanna-Barbera, plastic. PEZ Candy Inc., 1990s. Barney,
Fred, Pebbles, and Dino. Under 5" tall. $3-5 each.

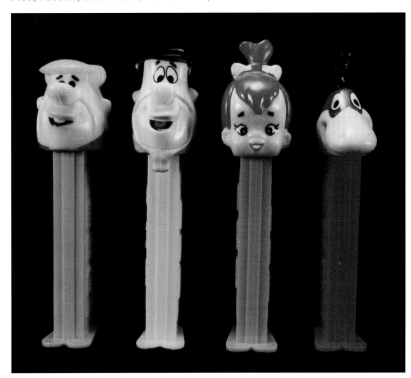

The Flintstones © Hanna-Barbera/Universal City Studios Inc., plastic. The
Topps Co., 1993. Fred and Dino riding in a car. 2" tall. $10-15.

The Flintstones © Hanna-Barbera/Universal City Studios Inc., plastic. Creative Confection Concepts, Inc., 1993. Caption: "Bedrock Bowl-O-Rama Jawbreaker." 3.5" tall. $3-5. *Courtesy of Donna Ambeau.*

The Flintstones © Hanna-Barbera/ Universal City Studios Inc., plastic. The Topps Co., 1993. Dino. 3.25" tall. $5-10.

The Flintstones © Hanna-Barbera/Universal City Studios Inc., plastic. The Topps Co., 1993. Fred. 2.5" tall. $5-10.

The Flintstones © Hanna-Barbera/Universal City Studios Inc., plastic. Creative Confection Concepts, Inc., 1993. Caption: "Bedrock Boulder Soft Center Rock Candy." 3.5" tall. $3-5. *Courtesy of Donna Ambeau.*

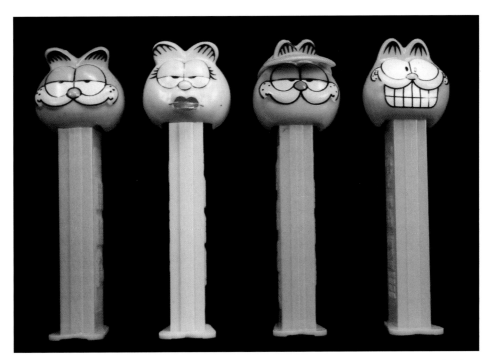

Garfield © Jim Davis/PAWS Inc., plastic. PEZ Candy Inc., 1980s. Garfield, Arlene, Garfield with visor, Garfield grinning. Under 5" tall. $5-10 each.

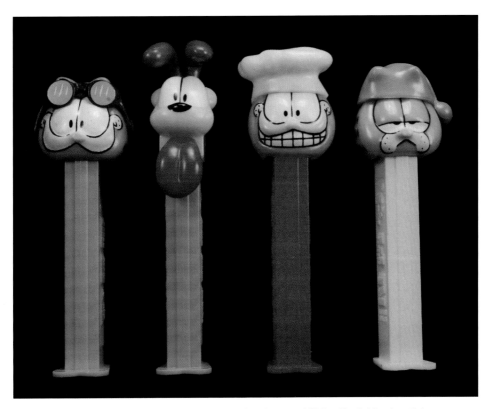

Garfield © Jim Davis/PAWS Inc., plastic. PEZ Candy Inc., 1990s. Garfield pilot, Odie, Garfield chef, Garfield sleepy. Under 5" tall. $3-5 each.

Garfield characters © Jim Davis/PAWS Inc., rubber. Amurol Confections Co., N/A. Caption: "Odie Suckers, Pooky Pops, Garfield Suckers." Peel off mold. 5.25" tall. $3-5 each. *Courtesy of Donna Ambeau.*

(The Real) Ghostbusters © Columbia Pictures Industries, Inc., plastic. Superior Toy & Mfg. Co., 1987. 2.75" tall. $5-10.

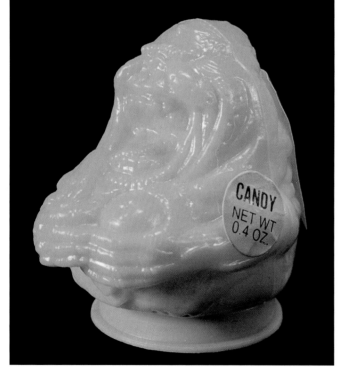

(The Real) Ghostbusters © Columbia Pictures Industries, Inc., plastic. The Topps Co., 1989. Slimer. 2" tall. . $5-10.

(The Real) Ghostbusters © Columbia Pictures Industries, Inc., plastic. Amurol Confections Co., 1984. Caption: "Slimer Bubble Gum." 5.75" long. $10-15. *Courtesy of Donna Ambeau.*

108

Gremlin © Warner Bros., plastic. The Topps Co., 1990. Remember – don't eat these candies after midnight! Gizmo. 1.75" tall. $15-20. *Courtesy of Donna Ambeau.*

Gremlin © Warner Bros., plastic. The Topps Co., 1990. Mohawk. 2" tall. $15-20.

Gremlin © Warner Bros., plastic. The Topps Co., 1990. 1.75" tall. $5-10.

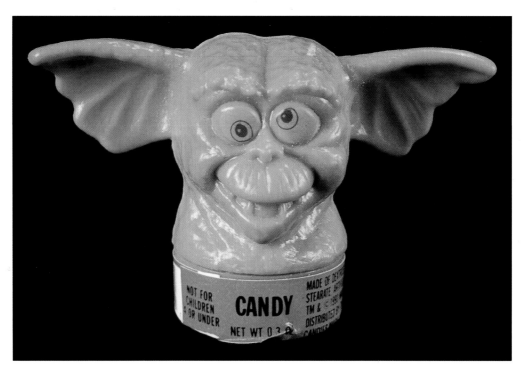

Gremlin © Warner Bros., plastic. The Topps Co., 1990. 2" tall. $5-10.

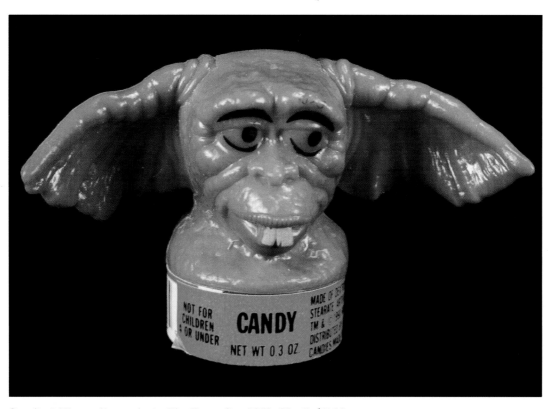

Gremlin © Warner Bros., plastic. The Topps Co., 1990. 2" tall. $5-10.

Hamburglar © McDonald's Corporation, plastic. Manufacturer unknown, 1998. McDonald's promotion. Six in the series. 3" tall. $1-3.

Holly Hobbie © American Greeting Corp., cardboard. Deran Confectionary/Borden Inc., 1988. Heart-shaped box. 5.5" tall. $10-15.

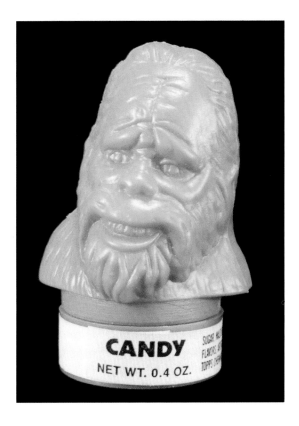

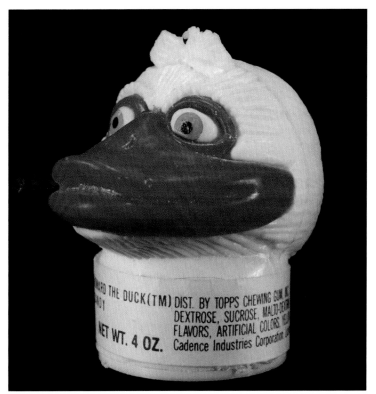

Howard the Duck © Marvel Comics, plastic. The Topps Co., 1986. 1.75" tall. $15-20.

Harry and the Hendersons © Universal Studios, plastic. The Topps Co., 1987. 2.25" tall. $15-20. *Courtesy of Donna Ambeau.*

Dinosaur, plastic wrap. The Topps Co, 1988. Caption: "Dino Dinosaur Toy with Candy Eggs." 2.75" tall. $5-10. *Courtesy of Donna Ambeau.*

Jurassic Park © Universal City Studios/Amblin Entertainment, Inc., plastic. The Topps Co, 1992. 2" tall. $5-10.

Jurassic Park © Universal City Studios/Amblin Entertainment, Inc., plastic. The Topps Co., 1992. Caption: "Jurassic Park Toy Dinosaur and Candy Inside." Egg. 3" tall. $3-5. *Courtesy of Donna Ambeau.*

Little Shop of Horrors © The Geffen Film Company, plastic. The Topps Co., 1986. Venus flytrap. 2.5" tall. $15-20. *Courtesy of Donna Ambeau.*

Jurassic Park © Universal City Studios, Inc./ Amblin, cardboard. Creative Confection Concepts Inc., 1992. Caption: "Jurassic Park. Wild Cherry Jawbreakers Raptor Bites. Tropical Fruit Jawbreakers Spitters." 5.5" tall. $10-15 each. *Courtesy of Donna Ambeau.*

Right:
Li'l Lion, plastic. PEZ Candy Inc., 1960s. Under 5" tall. $30-45. Yappy Dog, plastic. PEZ Candy Inc., 1970s. Under 5" tall. $50-75.

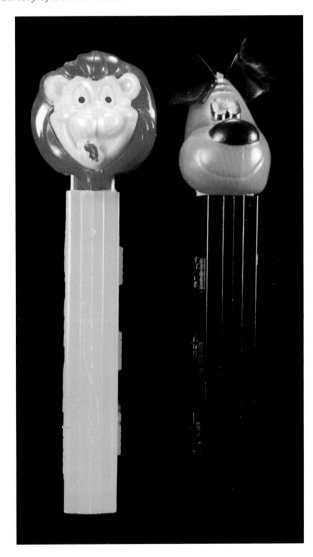

Looney Tunes © Warner Bros., plastic. PEZ Candy Inc., 1990s. Taz, Speedy, Yosemite Sam, Tweety, and Sylvester. Under 5" tall. $3-5 each.

Below:
Looney Tunes (Bugs Bunny) ©Warner Bros., plastic. PEZ Candy Inc., 1999. Caption: "Candy Pen." 6.25" tall. $5-10.

Looney Tunes © Warner Bros., plastic. Russell Stover Candies., 1997. Caption: "Haunted House." Bank. 5" tall. $10-15.

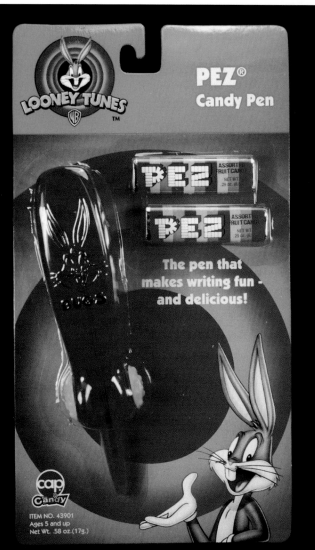

114

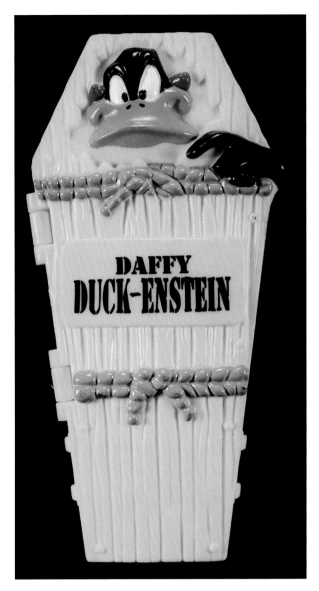

Looney Tunes (Daffy Duck) © Warner Bros., plastic.
Russell Stover Candies, 1997. Caption: "Daffy Duck-
Enstein." Musical. 6.25" tall. $15-20.

Looney Tunes (Bugs Bunny) © Warner Bros., plastic.
Russell Stover Candies, 1997. Caption: "Bugs Mummy."
Musical. 6.25" tall. $15-20.

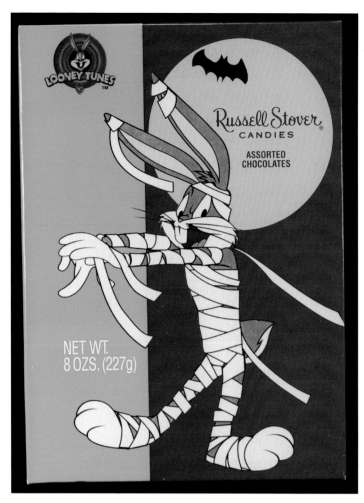

Looney Tunes © Warner Bros., cardboard. Russell Stover Candies, 1997. Bugs Bunny dressed as a mummy. 6.25" tall. $5-10.

Looney Tunes © Warner Bros., cardboard. Russell Stover Candies, 1997. Daffy Duck dressed as Frankenstein. 6.25" tall. $5-10.

Looney Tunes © Warner Bros., cardboard. Russell Stover Candies, 1997. Bugs Bunny and Daffy Duck with a Christmas theme. 4.5" tall. $5-10.

M&M © Mars Inc., plastic. Manufacturer unknown, 1997. Burger King promotion. Red M&M on raft. Five in series. 2" tall. $1-3.

M&M © Mars Inc., plastic. Manufacturer unknown, 1997. Burger King promotion. Blue M&M with saxophone. 3.25" tall. $1-3.

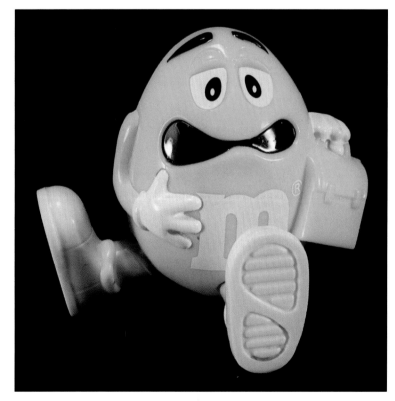

M&M © Mars Inc., plastic. Manufacturer unknown, 1997. Burger King promotion. Yellow M&M with lunchbox. Five in series. 2.5" tall. $1-3.

M&M © Mars Inc., plastic. Toyz 'n Treatz Inc., 2000.
Caption: "M&M's Time Capsule Kit." 10" tall. $10-15.

M&M © Mars Inc., plastic. OddzOn Inc.,
2000. Caption: "M&M's. Official Candy
of the New Millennium." 4" in diameter.
$5-10.

M&M © Mars Inc., plastic. OddzOn Inc.,
2000. Caption: "M&M's Minis Aircraft
Candy Carriers, Candy Rocket." 7.5" long.
$5-10.

M&M © Mars Inc., plastic. OddzOn Inc., N/A. Caption:
"M&M's Minis Rigs Candy Carriers." 6.5" long. $5-10.

M&M © Mars Inc., plastic. OddzOn Inc., N/A. Caption: "M&M's Racing Team
Candy Dispenser." 8.5" long. $10-15.

M&M © Mars Inc., plastic. Manufacturer unknown, 1997. Blue M&M playing
basketball. 12.75" tall. $15-20.

M&M © Mars Inc., plastic. Manufacturer unknown, 1996. Orange M&M playing baseball. 9.25" tall. $15-20.

M&M © Mars Inc., plastic. Manufacturer unknown, 2000. Caption: "M&M's La-Z-Boy Dispenser." Yellow M&M sitting in a chair. Limited edition. 9" tall. $15-20.

M&M © Mars Inc., plastic. OddzOn Inc., 1999. Orange M&M "Hide 'n Hander." 5.5" tall. $10-15.

M&M © Mars Inc., plastic. OddzOn Inc., 1999. Red M&M "Jammin' Red." 5.5" tall. $10-15.

Marvel Comic Character (X-Men) © Marvel Comics, plastic. Classic Heroes Inc., 1995.
Caption: "X-Men Laser Candy." 4" tall. $10-15.

Marvel Comic Character (Fantastic Four) © Marvel Comics Group, foil wrap. Amurol Confections Co., 1982. Caption: "Fantastic Four 100 Bubble Gum Chunks." 5.5" tall. $10-15. *Courtesy of Donna Ambeau.*

Marvel Comic Character (Iron Man) © Marvel Comics, plastic. Classic Heroes Inc., 1995. 4.25" tall. $5-10.

Marvel Comic Character (X-Men/Wolverine) © Marvel Comics, plastic. Classic Heroes Inc., 1995. 4" tall. $5-10.

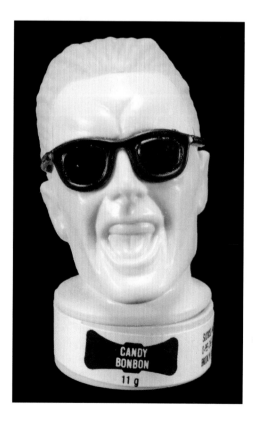

Marvel Comic Character (Fantastic Four/The Thing) © Marvel Comics, plastic. Classic Heroes Inc., 1995. 4" tall. $5-10.

Max Headroom © Chrysalis Visual Programming Ltd., plastic. The Topps co., 1987. 2.5" tall. $15-20.

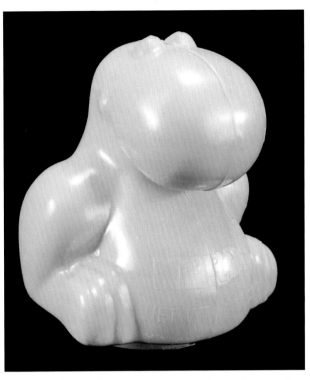

Mighty Morphin Power Rangers © Saban, plastic. The Topps Co., 1995. Kimberly. 2.25" tall. $5-10

Nerds © Willy Wonka Brands, plastic. Willy Wonka Brands, 1984. 2.25" tall. $5-10. *Courtesy of Donna Ambeau.*

The Muppets © Jim Henson Productions, plastic. PEZ Candy Inc., 1990s. Fozzie, Gonzo, Kermit, and Miss Piggy. Under 5" tall. $3-5 each.

Pluggo, plastic. The Topps Co., 1987. 2.25" tall. $5-10. *Courtesy of Donna Ambeau.*

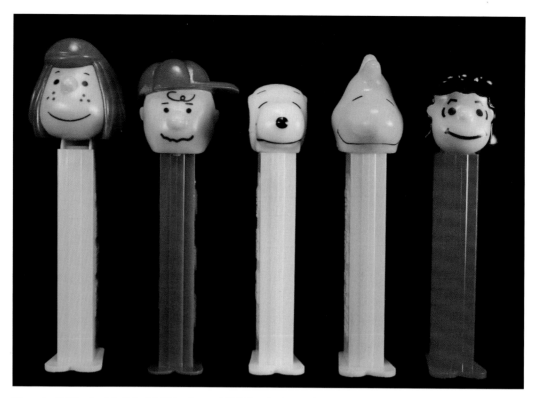

Peanuts © Charles M. Schulz/UFS, plastic. PEZ Candy Inc., 1990s. Peppermint Patty, Charlie Brown, Snoopy, Woodstock, and Lucy. Under 5" tall. $3-5 each. **Note:** A Charlie Brown dispenser was made with a frown expression. It is very hard to find.

Peanuts © Charles M. Schulz/UFS, plastic. The Dayton Hudson Corp., 2000. Caption: "Peanuts 50th Celebration." Snoopy on a doghouse. Complete with white scoop. 5.5" tall. $5-10.

Peanuts © Charles M. Schulz/UFS, plastic. Whitman's Candies, 1990s. Snoopy on an Easter egg. Bank. 5" tall. $10-15.

Peanuts © Charles M. Schulz/UFS, plastic. Whitman's Candies,
1990s. Snoopy on a pumpkin. Bank. 4.75" tall. $10-15.

Peanuts © Charles M. Schulz/UFS, plastic. Whitman's Candies,
1990s. Snoopy on a Christmas sled. Bank. 5" tall. $10-15.

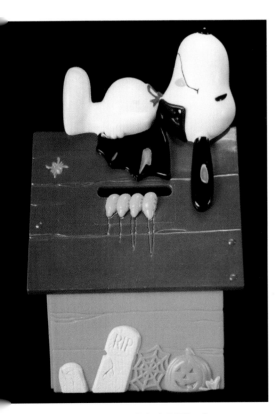

Peanuts © Charles M. Schulz/UFS, plastic.
Whitman's Candies, 1990s. Snoopy on a Halloween theme house. Bank. 6.25" tall. $10-15.

Peanuts © Charles M. Schulz/UFS, plastic. Galerie Au Chocolat, 2000. Caption:
"Peanuts 50th Celebration." Snoopy as a Flying Ace. 5" tall. $5-10.

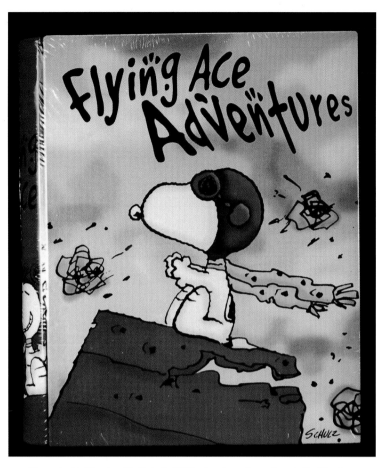

Peanuts © Charles M. Schulz/UFS, tin. American Specialty Confections, Inc., N/A. Snoopy as a Flying Ace. 6" tall. $10-15.

Peanuts © Charles M. Schulz/UFS, tin. Whitman's Candies, N/A. Snoopy dressed in a pumpkin costume. 5.5" tall. $10-15.

Peanuts © Charles M. Schulz/UFS, tin. Whitman's Candies, N/A. Snoopy dressed as Santa. 5.5" tall. $10-15.

Popeye © Elzie Segar/KFS, plastic. Superior Toy & Mfg. Co., 1983. Popeye with his can of spinach. 3.5" tall. $5-10.

Pluto © Walt Disney Co., plastic. Manufacturer unknown, N/A. Pluto with his dog dish. 3.5" tall. $5-10.

Pokemon characters (with keychain) © Nintendo/Bandai Co., plastic. OddzOn, Inc., 1999. Caption: "Jigglypuff, Poliwhirl, and Pikachu." 3.75" tall. $3-5 each. *Courtesy of Donna Ambeau.*

Powerpuff Girls © Cartoon Network, plastic. OddzOn Inc., 2001. Blossom. 4.25" tall. $3-5.

Pokemon © Nintendo/Bandai Co. Ltd., plastic. Amurol Confections Co., 1999. Caption: "Pikachu." 2.5" in diameter. $3-5. *Courtesy of Donna Ambeau.*

Powerpuff Girls © Cartoon Network, tin. Boston America Corp., 2000. Bubbles. 2.5" in diameter. $1-3.

Punkys © Willy Wonka Brands, cardboard. Willy Wonka Brands, 1986. Caption: "Punkys Ugly Tangy Speckled Candy Bites." 3.75" long. $10-15. *Courtesy of Donna Ambeau.*

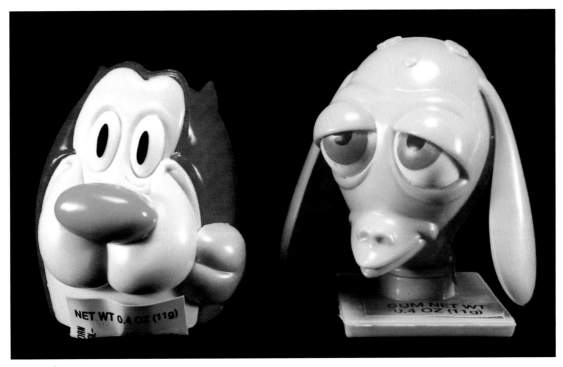

Ren and Stimpy © John Kricfalusi/Nickelodeon, plastic. The Topps Co., 1993. 2.25" tall. $5-10 each.

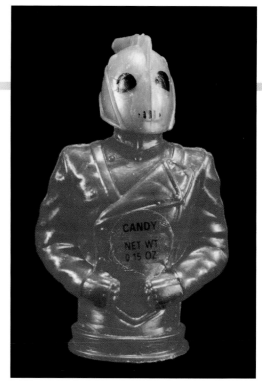

Rocketeer (half body) © The Walt
Disney Company, plastic. The Topps
Company, Inc., 1991. 2.5" tall. $5-10.

Rocketeer (face) © The Walt Disney Company, plastic. The
Topps Company, Inc., 1991. 2.25" tall. $5-10.

Rugrats © Klasky-Csupo Inc./Nickelodeon and Viacom International
Inc., tin. Frankford Candy & Chocolate Co., 1999. Angelica is holding
a bouquet of flowers. 7.5" tall (w/ handle). $10-15.

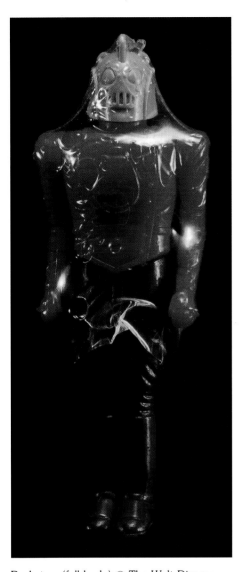

Rocketeer (full body) © The Walt Disney Company, plastic. The Topps Company, Inc., 1991. 5.25" tall. $5-10.

Rugrats © Klasky-Csupo Inc./Nickelodeon and Viacom International Inc., plastic. Amurol Confections Co., N/A. Caption: "Reptar Eggs." 3" tall. $10-15.

Scooby Doo © Hanna-Barbera/Cartoon Network, plastic. Houston Harvest Gift Products, 2000. Caption: "The Mystery Machine." 3.25" tall. $5-10.

The Simpsons © Matt Groening/Twentieth Century Fox Film Corporation, cardboard. Amurol Confections Co., 1990. Caption: "The Simpsons. 40 Sticks Bubble Gum." 2.75" tall. $10-15. *Courtesy of Donna Ambeau.*

Slush Puppie © Slush Puppie Corp., foil wrap. Amurol Confections Co., N/A. Caption: "Slush Puppie Paw Print Shaped Bubble Gum." 5" tall. $10-15. *Courtesy of Donna Ambeau.*

Star Wars © Lucasfilm, Ltd., plastic. PEZ Candy Inc., 1990s. Chewbacca, C3PO, Storm Trooper, Darth Vadar. Under 5" tall. $3-5 each.

Star Wars (Empire Strikes Back) © Lucasfilm, Ltd., plastic. The Topps co., 1980. Yoda and Boba Fett. 2.5" tall. $5-10 each.

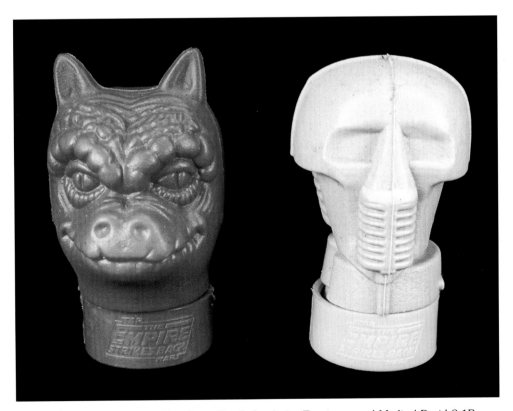

Star Wars (Empire Strikes Back) © Lucasfilm, Ltd., plastic. Tauntauns and Medical Droid 2-1B. 2.5" tall. $5-10 each.

Star Wars (Episode I) © Lucasfilm, Ltd., plastic.
OddzOn Inc., 1999. Caption: "Anakin Skywalker Film
Action Container." Complete with flicker trading card.
4.5" tall. $5-10 each.

Star Wars (Episode I) © Lucasfilm, Ltd., plastic.
OddzOn Inc., 1999. Caption: "R2-D2 Candy
Hander." 4.5" tall. $10-15.

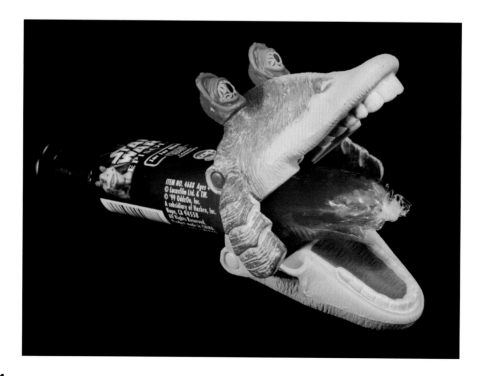

Star Wars (Episode I) ©
Lucasfilm, Ltd., plastic.
OddzOn, Inc., 1999. Jar Jar
Binks. Caption: "Monster
Mouth." 8.5" long. $3-5.
Courtesy of Donna Ambeau.

Star Wars (Episode I) © Lucasfilm, Ltd., plastic. OddzOn Inc., 1999. Caption: "Jar Jar Binks Candy Hander." 7" tall. $10-15.

Teenage Mutant Ninja Turtles © Mirage Studios, plastic. The Topps Co., 1991. Raphael. 4.75" tall. $5-10.

Star Wars (Episode I) © Lucasfilm, Ltd., plastic. OddzOn Inc., 1999. Caption: "Naboo Fighter Dispenser." 8.5" long. $10-15.

Teenage Mutant Ninja Turtles © Mirage Studios, plastic. The Topps Co., 1990. Leonardo. 2.75" tall. $5-10 . *Courtesy of Donna Ambeau.*

Teenage Mutant Ninja Turtles © Mirage Studios, plastic. Amurol Confections Co., 1991. Caption: "Teenage Mutant Ninja Turtles Fruit Candy. Tattoo Inside. Collect All 4." 2.5" in diameter. $5-10. *Courtesy of Donna Ambeau.*

Teenage Mutant Ninja Turtles © Mirage Studios, plastic wrap. Alma-Leo U.S.A., Inc., 1990. Caption: "Leo. Teenage Mutant Ninja Turtles Pizza Candy." 5.25" tall. $10-15. *Courtesy of Donna Ambeau.*

Tiny Toon Adventures © Warner Bros., plastic. The Topps Co., 1991. Buster and Babs. 3.5"
tall. $5-10. *Courtesy of Donna Ambeau.*

Tiny Toon Adventures © Warner Bros., plastic. The Topps Co., 1991. Plucky
and Hamilton. 2.75" tall. $5-10. *Courtesy of Donna Ambeau.*

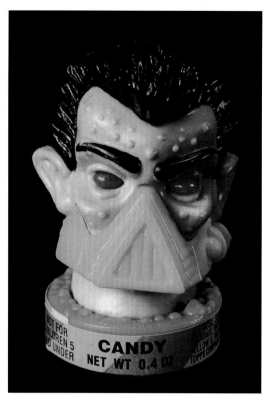

Toxic Crusader © Troma Inc., plastic. The Topps Co., 1991. Mask. 2.5" tall. $5-10.

Toxic Crusader © Troma Inc., plastic. The Topps Co., 1991. Big Nose. 2.25" tall. $5-10.

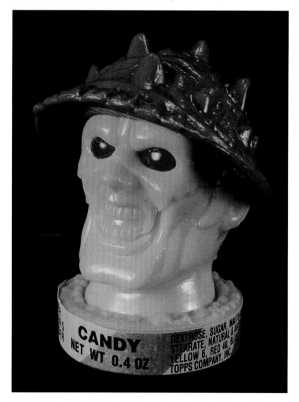

Toxic Crusader © Troma Inc., plastic. The Topps Co., 1991. Greenhat. 2.5" tall. $5-10.

Toxic Crusader © Troma Inc., plastic. The Topps Co., 1991. Pop Eye. 2" tall. $5-10.

Toy Story (Mr. Potato Head) © Walt Disney Co., Pixar, and Hasbro, Inc., plastic. OddzOn Inc., 1996. 3.5" tall. $5-10. *Courtesy of Donna Ambeau.*

Toy Story 2 (Rex) © Walt Disney Co. and Pixar. Manufacturer unknown, 1999. McDonald's promotion. Six in the series. 5.75" tall. $10-15.

Toy Story 2 (Woody & Bull's Eye) © Walt Disney Co. and Pixar. Manufacturer unknown, 1999. McDonald's promotion. Six in the series. Caption: "Hey howdy hey." 8" tall. $10-15.

Toy Story 2 (Buzz Lightyear) © Walt Disney Co. and Pixar. Tapper Candies Inc., 1999. Caption: "Candy Camera." 3.75" tall. $5-10.

Toy Story 2 (Buzz Lightyear) © Walt Disney Co. and Pixar. Tapper Candies Inc., 1999. Caption: "Spaceship." 4.75" long. $5-10.

Sonic the Hedgehog © Sega Enterprises, Inc., plastic. The Topps Co., 1993. Sonic's arms are moveable. 3.5" tall. $15-20. *Courtesy of Donna Ambeau.*

Video game © Nintendo of America, Inc., plastic. Amurol Confections Co., 1993. Caption: "Game Boy Bubble Gum + Trading Cards." 4.25" tall. $3-5. *Courtesy of Donna Ambeau.*

Video game © Sega Enterprises, Inc., plastic. Amurol Confections Co., 1994. Caption: "Sonic the Hedgehog Bubble Gum Plus Sonic Trading Cards." 4.5" long. $5-10. *Courtesy of Donna Ambeau.*

Link © Nintendo of America Inc., plastic. The Topps Co., 1989. 3.25" tall. $10-15. *Courtesy of Donna Ambeau.*

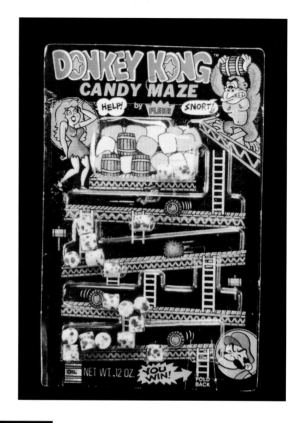

Arcade game, plastic/cardboard. Fleer Corp., 1981. Caption: "Donkey Kong Candy Maze © Nintendo of America, Inc." 5.5" tall. $15-20. *Courtesy of Donna Ambeau.*

Arcade games, cardboard. The Topps Co., 1981-1983. Video arcade gum series. Caption: "Donkey Kong © Nintendo of America, Inc., Frogger © Sega Enterprises, Inc., and Zaxxon © Sega Enterprises, Inc." 4" tall. $20-25 each. *Courtesy of Donna Ambeau.*

Bibliography

Braun, Debra S. *Collectibles Magazine*. New York, New York: Goodman Media Group, Fall 2000.

Brenner, Joël Glenn. *The Emperors of Chocolate: Inside the Secret World of Hershey and Mars*. New York, New York: Random House, Inc., 1999.

Brown, Andrea Lynn. *Country Collectibles Magazine*. New York, New York: Harris Publications, Spring 2001.

Brush, Jack and William Miller. *Modern Candy Containers & Novelties*. Paducah, Kentucky: Collector Books, 2001.

Clevenger, Patsy. *The Collector's World of M&Ms*. Atglen, Pennsylvania: Schiffer Publishing, Ltd., 1998.

Dezso, Douglas M., J. Leon Poirier, and Rose D. Poirier. *Collector's Guide to Candy Containers*. Paducah, Kentucky: Collector Books, 1998. *Note:* This is an excellent resource for identifying glass reproductions.

Editor. *Candy Containers – A Price Guide*. Gas City, Indiana: L-W Incorporated, 1996.

Eikelberner, George and Serge Agadjanian. *American Glass Candy Containers and More American Glass Candy Containers*. Belle Mead, New Jersey: Self published, 1968, 1970.

_____. *More American Glass Candy Containers*. Belle Mead, New Jersey: Self published, 1970.

_____. *Compleat American Candy Containers Handbook*. Mentor, Ohio: Bowden Publishing, 1986.

Geary, Richard. *PEZ Collectibles*. Atglen, Pennsylvania: Schiffer Publishing, Ltd., 1997.

Heuer, Ann Rooney. *American Country Collectibles Magazine*. New York, New York: Goodman Media Group, Winter 2000.

Korbeck, Sharon. *Toy Shop Magazine*. Iola, Wisconsin: Krause Publications, Bi Weekly Distribution 2000-2001.

Long, Jennie. *An Album of Candy Containers Volume I and II*. Kingsburg, California: Self published.

Matthews, Robert T. *A Collection of Old Glass Candy Containers*. Gleneig, Maryland: Self-published.

_____. *Antiquers of Glass Candy Containers*. Gleneig, Maryland: Self-published.

Stanley, Mary Louise. *A Century of Glass Toys – The "Sweetest" Memories of American Childhood*. Manchester, Vermont: Forward's Color Productions, Inc., 1970s.

Auction Websites:
www.100topauctionsites.com
www.ebay.com
www.yahoo.com

Candy Related Websites:
www.bubblegum.com (Amurol Confections)
www.pez.com (Pez Candy Inc.)
www.topps.com/Confectionery/conf_history.html
    (Topps Co., Inc.)
www.m-ms.com (M&M's Network)
www.oddzon.com (OddzOn/Cap Candy)
www.chase-goldenberg.com/capcandy.htm (OddzOn/
    Cap Candy)
www.comptons.com/encyclopedia/ARTICLES/0025/
    00393728_A.html (Fleer Corp.)
www.candycontainer.org (The Candy Container Col-
    lectors of America)

Candy Replacement Parts and Closures:

Tin/Aluminum
    Mike & Jo Baldwin
    P.O. Box 2971
    Anderson, Indiana 46018
    Phone (765) 643-7065

Paper
    Bob & Linda Kemig
    2216 Deerfield Place
    Bartlesville, Oklahoma 74006-8802
    Phone (918) 335-3265

Wood
    Chuck & Belva Adams
    3540 Richmond Road
    Lincoln, Nebraska 68504-1856
    Phone (402) 464-7715